x

MOSCOW and the WEST

S. F. Platonov

MOSCOW

AND THE

WEST

TRANSLATED AND EDITED BY

Joseph L. Wieczynski

INTRODUCTION BY

Serge A. Zenkovsky

ACADEMIC INTERNATIONAL

1972

RUSSIAN SERIES • VOLUME 9

Sergei F. Platonov   MOSCOW AND THE WEST

Translation of *Moskva i zapad* (Leningrad, 1925)

English translation and special contents of this edition copyright © 1972 by Academic International. All rights reserved, including the right to reproduce this book or any portions thereof in any form, by any means or for any purpose.

Library of Congress Catalog Card Number: 72-142000
ISBN: 0-87569-019-X
A Catalog Card follows the Index

Printed in the United States of America

ACADEMIC INTERNATIONAL • *publishers*
Box 666 • Hattiesburg • Mississippi • 39401

To the memory of our son
Stephen Christopher Wieczynski
my wife and I dedicate this work

CONTENTS

Map	vi
Introduction	vii
Preface	xviii
Author's Introduction	xxi

THE SIXTEENTH CENTURY AND THE TIME OF TROUBLES	**1**
THE FIRST HALF OF THE SEVENTEENTH CENTURY	**49**
THE SECOND HALF OF THE SEVENTEENTH CENTURY	**97**

Notes to the Introduction	142
Notes to the Text	144
Glossary	158
Index	161
Catalog Card	171

INTRODUCTION

In the present work, *Moscow and the West,* Sergei Fedorovich Platonov (1860-1933) offers a vivid and painstakingly scholarly discussion of Russia's modernization and her gradual return to the European cultural community during the sixteenth and seventeenth centuries. Platonov was a leading professor of Russian history at the University of St. Petersburg and one of the most distinguished members of the Russian Academy of Sciences. He specialized in the Muscovite period and was without a doubt the best qualified scholar to treat this exciting and intricate era of Russia's past. Since his outstanding book, published originally in 1925, was written primarily for Russian readers, this new foreward is intended to clarify some aspects of Russia's early historical evolution for Western students of today.

In the above paragraph the words, Russia's "gradual return to the European cultural community," have been used deliberately in order to stress the fact that Russia's establishment of relations with the nations of Western Europe in the sixteenth and seventeenth centuries and her integration into a more or less homogeneous European cultural world were primarily the reactivization of ancient ties. It should also be kept in mind that modernization—or, as it was often called, the "Westernization"—of Russia did not mean as drastic a change in her cultural patterns as has been the case more recently during the Westernization of many African and Asian nations. Indeed, the earliest history of present Russian territory reveals its close contacts with ancient Greco-Roman civilization. Long before the Slavs appeared in the East European plains an active cultural and economic intercourse existed between the populations of the South Russian prairie and the numerous Greek colonies established along the northern shore of the

Black Sea as early as the eighth century B. C. Later, at the beginning of our era, the frontier of the Roman Empire advanced to the southern provinces of the present Soviet Union.

The very Christianization of the Eastern Slavs in the late tenth century A. D. meant their inclusion in medieval European Christian civilization. It is true that Christianity came to them not from Rome but from Byzantium, but it reached the Slavs before the dissolution of the unity between the Western and Eastern churches when Byzantium, or the "Eastern Roman Empire," was still the luminary for all of Europe. Some Catholic historians even claim that Western missionaries went to the Russians before the arrival among them of the Greeks.

In the early centuries of Russian history close trade and dynastic ties existed between the West European states and Russia. Kiev and Regensburg were important terminal markets of east-west trade. A constant flow of goods between Novgorod and the Baltic ports of Germany and Scandinavia was a vital feature of North European economic activity. Russian princes and princesses married members of the royal dynasties of France, Germany, England, Hungary, Scandinavia and other countries. Among such marriages should be mentioned those of Anne and Elizabeth, daughters, and Eupraxia-Adelheid, a granddaughter, of the Kievan prince, Yaroslav (1019-1054). Anne, who married Henry I (1031-1060), the king of France, functioned as regent for her royal son, Philip II, and was the only literate member of the French royal family. The Norwegian king, Harald of Hardrara, who was killed shortly before Hastings in the battle of Stamford Bridge in England in 1066, for years courted and finally married Yaroslav's other daughter, Elizabeth. Eupraxia-Adelheid in 1029 became empress of the Holy Roman Empire of the German Nation during the fateful years of the investiture struggle between Henry IV and Pope Gregory VII. The family of the last Anglo-Saxon king, Harold, found refuge in Russia after the Norman invasion of England. The daughter of this unfortunate ruler around 1079 married the Russian prince, Vladimir Monomakh (1113-1125). Monomakh, whose father spoke five foreign languages, was the grandson of the Byzantine Emperor Constantine IX (1042-1055). Half a century earlier the children of another Anglo-Saxon king, Edmund Ironside (died in 1016), also lived as

Introduction

emigres at the Kievan court.[1] Many foreigners from southern, northern and western Europe resided in Kiev, Novgorod and other Russian cities. It may be added that religious tensions between Orthodox Russia and the Catholic West were almost unknown before the thirteenth century, while cultural differences between these two integral parts of medieval European civilization were rather insignificant.

The situation changed drastically during the thirteenth century. The Mongol conquest of Russia radically curtailed contact with the West. At the same time militant German knights of the Teutonic and Livonian Orders seized the southeastern Baltic shores. Exploiting the weakening of Russia to their benefit, Lithuania and Poland annexed most of Russia's western territories. Soon after, the Ottoman Empire gained control of the Black Sea and most of southeastern Europe. For centuries all these powers did their best to obstruct any development of Russian trade or renewal of Russia's prior relations with the West in order to keep the Russian principalities feeble and prevent their political expansion. Thus, by the beginning of the fourteenth century a virtual blockade was established around Russian territories, isolating them from Western Europe.

It should also be kept in mind that the very geographical position of medieval Russia almost necessarily led to isolation from the rest of the Christian world. With the exception of a narrow marshy band on the Baltic coast, which had no natural harbor, medieval Russia had no access to sea routes since its territory was restricted at that time primarily to the forests of the upper Volga River and its tributaries. Russia's population consequently was condemned to protracted economic and cultural stagnation and prevented from renewing former ties with the rest of the Christian world. The absence of mineral wealth, together with the agricultural poverty of northeastern Europe, were equally instrumental in retarding the economic growth of early Muscovite Russia.

Quite often the opinion is expressed that Eastern Christianity was responsible for the cultural and intellectual isolation of medieval Russia. Allegedly, Byzantium promoted religious intolerance and incited Russians against the countries of the Catholic world. Strangely enough, however, the same Eastern Orthodox Church did not prevent some other peoples—for instance, the Greeks themselves—from maintaining commercial and intellectual contacts with the West, even while under the Turkish yoke. Unlike the Russians, the Greeks, thanks to their favorable maritime location, remained one of the leading trading and seafaring peoples of the Mediterranean. Russia's continental position, in contrast, handicapped its economic, cultural and political interchange with medieval Western Europe. In consequence, Russia did not develop a mercantile tradition connecting it with the West and hence could not benefit from the fruits of intellectual progress which became particularly significant in the West during the Renaissance and Reformation.

Russia's fourteenth century was probably the time of her greatest isolation. Still, even in this "Dark Age" there were some economic bonds with the rest of Europe. Novgorod continued to serve as a trade outlet with the northern European markets; but this exchange, unfortuantely for Russia, had a peculiar, one-sided aspect. The Hanse monopolized Novgorod's export and import trade and, while the German merchants were steady guests in this important northern city, they allowed practically no Russians to send products abroad independently or to travel for business purposes to the West.

About the same phenomenon could be observed in southern trade at this time. Italian merchants from the Crimea—where Genoa had colonies until the end of the fifteenth century—would come to Russia offering merchandise from the Occident and Orient. Their excellent commerical organization, like that of the Hanse traders, hindered Russians from access in any significant numbers to the markets of the Black Sea.[2]

Yet cultural contacts were maintained with dying Byzantium and, after its fall, with the Near Eastern Orthodox churches. Russian bishops and monks often travelled to Constantinople, Mt. Athos and the Holy Land, and the Russian religious and artistic revival of the late fourteenth and fifteenth centuries, so closely connected with the names of Saints Sergius of Radonezh and Nilus of Sora (Nil Sorsky), testifies to the penetration into Russia of new spiritual ideas from the Greek world of the Near East. The Ottoman conquest of the Balkans also caused some migration of artists and writers from Greece and from

Introduction

among the Balkan Slavs to Moscow and other Russian cities. The paintings of Theophanos the Greek, Andrew Rublev and Dionysius were evidence of an artistic Renaissance on the Russian plains. The writings of Epiphany the Wise, Pakhomius Logofet, Sofonia of Riazan and their contemporaries, as well as a powerful monastic movement in North Russia, witness a very considerable reactivization of Russian cultural life—which some modern historians have called a "Russian pre-Renaissance."

Modern research has removed the impression of intellectual stagnation in feudal and Muscovite Russia. An outstanding contemporary historian of Russian literature, Professor Dmitry Tschizhevsky—who can hardly be suspected of pro-Muscovite bias—speaks of Russian literary and intellectual development in the fifteenth to seventeenth centuries as an era of spiritual and religious conflicts and struggles.[3] Indeed, Tschizhevsky was perfectly justified in making such a statement. In 1370-1420 the strong heretical movement of the Strigolniki was observed in Novgorod and Pskov. This was not solely a heresy but rather a new way of thinking, a new approach to the problems of the relations between God and man, the power of the church and the right of the church to control thought. One hundred years later the very similar movement of the so-called "Judaizers" likewise grew in Novgorod, whence it spread to Moscow. Even such highly placed spiritual and political leaders as Metropolitan Zosima, head of the Russian Orthodox Church, and Ivan III himself, who is usually considered the first Russian autocrat, were accused of succumbing to this new "heresy." Many recent investigators of the Judaizers feel that this movement, too, was not merely an expression of opposition to the teaching of the church but rather the spreading of humanistic ideas and the development of a more critical approach to the church and to traditional culture. To some extent the preaching of these Russian Judaizers was even more radical than that of their "heretical" Western contemporaries. In several aspects their bold tenets remind us of the teaching of the Unitarians, who came into being in the West about a hundred years later. The origin of these movements is unclear; but, since they resemble to some extent certain "heresies" in Western Europe, it can be presumed that their development was the result of the close contact of Novgorod and Pskov with the West. On the other hand, there are indications that at least the heresy of the Judaizers was of southern origin.

During the sixteenth century several other new intellectual and religious movements arose in Muscovite Russia. While most of them were stifled by the government and reactionary elements of the clergy, their appearance clearly testifies to a continuous fermentation of thought in Old Muscovy. We now know that more Russians travelled to the West in the sixteenth century than was supposed only fifty years ago. We are also aware that West European knowledge continuously filtered into Muscovy. Since the beginning of the sixteenth century considerable information on the geography and the history of Western Europe was included in the Russian chronicles and chronographs. Toward the end of this century William Camden's *Britania,* which contained wide information on the British Isles, was translated in Moscow. In 1564 and 1568 there appeared Russian translations of the *Chronicle of the Entire World* by the Polish historian, Martin Bielski, and the books of foreigners who travelled to Russia—such as Herberstein, Olearius and other Western works—were also rendered into Russian for use by Muscovite diplomats and statesmen. Fedor Karpov (died before 1545), until recently a rather forgotten literary figure of the early sixteenth century, showed in his writings that he was acquainted with Latin and Greek *belles lettres.*

Keeping in mind these cultural and spiritual currents in medieval Russia, one can see now with different eyes the intellectual conditions in Old Muscovy. It was spiritually much less homogenous and intellectually less static than many historians thought half a century ago.

Russians realized very early the necessity for adjusting to the more progressive civilization of the West. Hardly was a unified Russian state created by Ivan III (1462-1505) when Russian statesmen displayed an understanding of the need to resume ties with the West. Ivan III was the first Russian ruler to begin the struggle for a window on Europe in the Baltic area. Most sovereigns who followed him continued his effort to open up direct communication with the West European world.

In *Moscow and the West* Platonov presents a clear picture of the

Introduction

various difficulties connected with a renewal of this communication. Russia's foreign enemies, who had blockaded the Russians since the thirteenth century—Swedes, Germans of the Livonian Order, Poles and Turks—were not alone in attempting to undermine all Russian efforts to gain the fruits of Western culture and technological development. Among the Russians themselves there were numerous conservative elements, especially in the aristocracy and church, who were opposed to cultural changes, fearing that such changes would undermine their control of society.

The continuous efforts of the Muscovite government to modernize the country, and the reaction of the conservative groups to these efforts, form the heart of Platonov's masterful presentation of the cultural changes which were transforming seventeenth-century Russia. This great Russian historian was a staunch believer in an enlightened Russian monarchy as it developed after the reforms of Peter the Great. Although his main academic work was done in the history of sixteenth and seventeenth-century Muscovite Russia, his interest in his country's past never permitted him to approach this period uncritically. Yet perhaps even he underestimated the cultural changes taking place at that time. The observation of recent trends in Asia and Africa, for example, raises the question of approaching this early period of Russia's Westernization in a way slightly different from that of Platonov. It should be kept in mind that he was born over a century ago, when Russia was actually the only country to undergo the effect of Westernization. In our time, when most countries of the world outside Europe and North America have had to modernize their structure and adjust their cultures and economic lives to the pattern of the rapidly developing West, historians have better opportunity to understand the process of cultural shifts. One can see now what tremendous obstacles this adjustment encountered, even in most recent years, despite all advancements of communication and in industrial and agricultural technology.

The present writer would like to add that in his opinion Platonov perhaps also underestimated the continuous effort of Tsar Alexis (1645-1676) to obtain a firm foothold on the Baltic Sea. Had he been successful he would have opened a window onto Western Europe a half century before his son, Peter the Great. Moreover, Alexis showed no hesitation in bringing to Moscow well-educated monks from Kiev, to whom he entrusted even the education of his own children, as well as foreign technicians and foreign military specialists. Dying in 1676 at the age of 46, Alexis lived too short a time to see the fruits of his labor, and encountered too many obstacles effectively to modernize his country. Moreover, it was not until his reign that the economy of Russia began to gather strength. The integration of Siberia into the Russian tsardom provided very considerable resources for the rehabilitation of the economy and treasury. The development of trade through the White Sea and the steady growth of foreign settlement in Moscow during the reign of Alexis permitted a wider penetration of new technology, new military techniques and new ideas. Thus it fell to Alexis' son, Peter, to harvest the fruits of Russia's continental expansion and of the concerted work of his father, who prepared the ground for Russia's modernization.

Hardly anyone other than Platonov could have presented such a concise and penetrating analysis of the eventful changes in Russian cultural life and politics from the fifteenth to seventeenth centuries. Unusual command of source materials, deep perception of historical processes and clear, precise language permitted him to give in *Moscow and the West* a brilliant picture of the three centuries of evolution of Muscovite Russia.

Sergei F. Platonov was the last of the great pre-revolutionary Russian historians. Although he never wrote a multi-volume history of Russia as did Sergei M. Soloviev and Vasily O. Kliuchevsky, scholars usually rank him in the same category as these two leading Russian historiographers. Born in 1860, he graduated rather early — at the age of twenty-one — from the University of St. Petersburg, where he studied under Professor Constantine N. Bestuzhev-Riumin, the founder of the St. Petersburg school of historiography and an outstanding specialist in medieval Russian chronicles and archives. This school paid particular attention to the critical investigation and the publication of original source material. In 1888, only seven years after his graduation, Platonov himself became a professor at this university, and steadily ascended in his academic career until almost the last year of his life. His first major publication

Introduction

was of seventeenth-century historical source materials, *Old Russian Writings on the Time of Troubles* (St. Petersburg, 1888). Characteristically for him, he did not limit himself in this work to an evaluation of this material's historical importance for early seventeenth-century Russia. He analysed it from a literary point of view as well and offered penetrating characterizations of the writers themselves. Platonov's main work, *Essays on the History of the Time of Troubles in the Muscovite State in the Sixteenth and Seventeenth Centuries (An Attempt to Study the Social Structure and Relations of the Classes in the Time of Trouble)* (St. Petersburg, 1899),[4] was devoted to the same period. In several respects he followed in this study the traditions of his great predecessors, Soloviev and Kliuchevsky, paying considerable attention to the role of the state in Russian history. At the same time, however, he carefully analysed the social conditions and conflicts in Old Russia. Platonov proposed in this study his own original interpretation of Ivan IV's "oprichnina," which he saw as primarily a tool in Ivan's hands for destroying the powerful upper aristocracy of feudal Russia and promoting the small service gentry. In this book Platonov was also the first to differentiate various stages of the Time of Troubles and stress the social fermentation during these first Russian revolutionary events.

Two other works by S. F. Platonov, *History of Russia*, written for the high schools, and *Lectures on Russian History*, which was intended primarily for university students, became the standard textbooks for secondary and higher institutions of education for a quarter of a century. Both deeply influenced two generations of educated Russians and are still used in the original by Russian emigre schools abroad or in translation in many countries, including the United States.[5]

The study of Russian history made Platonov—grandson of a serf and son of a worker—a firm but enlightened conservative and a convinced supporter of the Russian monarchy. He had little respect for the revolutionary movement, which he considered would bring catastrophe upon his country. In his university textbook on Russian history he did not hesitate to call the Decembrist revolt of 1825—considered by representatives of the intelligentsia to be the beginning of a new and enlightened era in Russian intellectual life—a "criminal conspiracy" and "rebellion and riots." He admitted frankly that he was a staunch individualist and deeply disliked any collective enterprise in scholarship.

Unexpectedly, the October revolution did not immediately interrupt Platonov's career. In 1918 he became chairman of the Archeological Commission and in 1920 he was elected to membership in the prestigious Russian Academy of Sciences. From 1920 until 1925 he was the director of the library of that Academy, and in 1925-1928 he served as director of the Pushkin House (Pushkinskii dom), an institute for the study of Russian literature within the Academy of Sciences. Finally, in 1928, he was appointed chairman of the commission for the publication of Alexander Pushkin's works. Platonov was even permitted to travel to Western Europe, where he met his emigre daughter and her family in Paris. Perhaps this last trip led to his downfall, for in 1931 he was abruptly expelled from the Academy of Sciences because of his "conservative and monarchist ideas." The next year he was arrested and deported to Samara, a minor provincial city on the lower Volga, where he resided in freedom but in humble circumstances, under the supervision of the political police. On January 16, 1933, he died there.

A recent Soviet publication admits that Platonov's historical concepts considerably influenced pre-revolutionary and even Soviet historiography.[6] Contemporary Russian historians sometimes accept his conclusions, sometimes slightly modify them, or sometimes hide them behind the screen of official rhetoric and terminology; but his explanations of the events of the times of Ivan IV, Boris Godunov and the beginning of the seventeenth century still figure prominently in their books.

Platonov's knowledge of the sixteenth and early seventeenth centuries was proverbial. His analyses were clear, cautious and scrupulously verified. His writings, although colorful and saturated with the expressions and sayings of bygone days, were nonetheless exact and always moulded in elegant and precise language. His lively and popular lectures were heavily attended not only by history students but by students from other disciplines, as well. Those who studied under him in St. Petersburg University admired his easy, witty and expressive way of presenting, discussing, and analysing Russia's past, and he is remembered with great warmth. Once or twice a month, as Professor George V.

Introduction

Vernadsky, now Professor Emeritus of Yale University, has remembered,[7] on Wednesdays Platonov would hold open house for his friends, colleagues, assistants and advanced students. At these soirees a wide range of artistic, literary, historical and political questions would be discussed. His examinations, always oral, were rather short but demanding. Professor Vladimir Weidlé, the well-known art historian, recalls a former colleague who went not very well prepared to take his examination with Platonov. The latter asked several questions, attentively listened to the answers, and then quietly told the student: "Please, better come back another time. I realize that you have read all the right pages of my textbook. I hope that by the next time you will have also read all of the left ones."[8]

* * *

A translation of Professor S. F. Platonov's writings presents some rather uncommon difficulties. His language is suffused with terminology, quotations and sayings of the writers and statesmen of Old Russia. The translation of such a rich text is extremely complex. Old English terminology cannot be substituted for the Russian in view of the dissimilar political and social structures of the two societies, vast differences in the mentalities of the Russian and English contemporaries of Ivan the Terrible and Henry VIII, and finally, because of the stylistic differences between these two languages in the sixteenth and seventeenth centuries.

Therefore, in order to translate this text, readily understandable to a Russian historian but not easy for an English-speaking person, the translator had to interpret, as much as to translate, the Old Russian terms and expressions into modern English. Perhaps this requirement to some extent deprives Platonov's original text of its colorful and variegated shadings but it makes the translation more exact and accessible to contemporary American students of Old Muscovy's relations with the West. The translator is to be congratulated for his successful accomplishment of this task.

Serge A. Zenkovsky

Vanderbilt University

PREFACE

It was with no small sense of misgiving that I agreed to undertake the first English translation of Platonov's *Moskva i Zapad*. Those who have read the original will readily recognize the difficulty of such an endeavor. Native Russians have found great enchantment in these pages. Platonov's somewhat archaic style and his frequent citation of passages and isolated words and phrases from sixteenth and seventeenth century sources evoke the written language and the spirit of the period he examines. One feels that he is reading a work composed by one or another of the historical personages whom Platonov develops in his narrative. To reproduce such a style in another tongue, to capture the rich flavor of the original, is impossible for any translator. Anyone who renders Platonov's work into another language must be prepared to suffer a certain degree of disenchantment with his product.

For this reason I have set modest limits for myself. My intention was simply to reproduce Platonov's text in the clearest, most direct English possible. Nor is this objective alien to Platonov's own intention, for with all his imagery and color he practiced a simplicity and directness that any historian must envy. When I have had to choose between fidelity to his lyricism and accuracy of meaning, I have invariably chosen the latter. I have taken the one liberty of dividing his longer paragraphs and sentences into segments more palatable to the English reader. Comments that appear within brackets in the text are my own. All parenthetical material is the author's.

In editing this work I have attempted to keep my identifications and commentary to a minimum. Terms that are clarified by their use in the text and personalities that are sufficiently identified in the narrative receive no further elucidation. The reader is directed to the glossary of special Russian terminology at the end of this work for identification of specialized terminology in Platonov's text. In some instances I have relied upon internal editing of the text to clarify Platonov's meaning. Thus I have at times supplied first names and patronymics for personalities the author identifies only by initials, dates of major reigns and events and other illustrative data. The system of transliteration is basically that of the Library of Congress, with certain modifications. Ligatures I have omitted completely. As a concession to the reader I have rendered the initial Russian diphthongs as "ya" and "yu," not as "ia" and "iu." Endings of Russian names have been reproduced as "y," not as "i" or "ii." Many proper Russian names I have anglicized (Peter, Michael, Alexis, Sophia), as well as a few Russian historical terms that are sufficiently well known to students of Russian institutions (boiars, archimandrite, etc.). I have retained Polish and other non-Russian names in their original national spelling (thus Niemojewski, not Nemoevsky). In general I have omitted the Russian soft sign when it precedes a vowel, particularly in reproducing proper names.

There are many friends to whom I owe debts of gratitude, not only for assisting me in producing this work, but in furthering my professional development. The two chairmen under whom I have initiated my career as a teacher and researcher, Professor Robert G. Landen (now of the University of South Carolina) and Professor James I. Robertson, Jr. (at present Chairman of the Department of History at Virginia Polytechnic Institute and State University) have encouraged my efforts and inspired me by their own great gifts of scholarship. Mrs. Wolter J. Fabrycky of Blacksburg, Virginia offered many helpful suggestions on translation of difficult passages of the text. Professor Peter von Wahlde first conceived this project and encouraged its completion, while offering important suggestions of his own. Mrs. Carolyn Alls, secretary of the History Department of Virginia Polytechnic Institute and State University, typed part of the manuscript and has made my life as a writer easier in innumerable ways. Mr. and Mrs. Joseph M. Ward of Silver Spring, Maryland provided welcome and valuable hospitality during my research trips to the Library of Congress. The American Philosophical Society has awarded me two grants which, although they were not intended to support this present project, greatly facilitated my study of early Russian history. Professor John T. Alexander of the University of Kansas deserves special recognition. He has read the manuscripts and offered many valuable suggestions and emendations. His own translation of another of Platonov's works, *The Time of Troubles* (Lawrence, 1970), is to my mind one of the finest renditions of a classic work of Russian history into English. Mistakes that remain are, of course, my own.

Finally, I must express my deep gratitude to my wife, Jo. She has been my companion since the first days of graduate study and has assisted me not only by her considerable skill in matters editorial, but with encouragement and assurance. In our marriage she has provided the order, serenity and beauty that every writer needs. This book, like all my work, is as much hers as mine.

Joseph L. Wieczynski

Blacksburg, Virginia
February, 1971

AUTHOR'S INTRODUCTION

In conceiving this work the author did not pretend to provide an exhaustive study of the complicated and not fully explored problem of the Europeanization of Russia. His objective was to show the main features of this cultural process. For material he has relied upon the group of scholarly surveys from which his own university course has been composed. The author will feel fully satisfied if he inspires readers with the conviction that the link between Muscovite Russia and the European West was formed earlier and was stronger than has usually been thought. For this reason the author has devoted most of his exposition to the earlier epochs.

MOSCOW and the WEST

Chapter One

THE SIXTEENTH CENTURY AND TIME OF TROUBLES

I   The Tale of the Knight Poppel. Foreigners in Moscow Before the Time of Ivan the Terrible

We must cease believing the old tale that in the year 1486 a certain German knight, Poppel, who had been wandering through regions remote from and poorly known in Europe, somehow reached Russia and, upon his return home, told the Holy Roman Emperor, Frederick III, of Moscow as though it were his own political and geographical discovery. The Emperor, supposedly startled by his account of the might of Russia, then sent this same Poppel to Moscow to request of Grand Prince Ivan III the hand of his daughter for Frederick's nephew and to reward the Russian prince in return with the title of king.[1] During his second visit to Moscow in 1488 Poppel himself boasted that only through him had Germany learned of the power and riches of "the noble and wise sovereign," Ivan III. But this boast was empty and false. It testifies to Poppel's frivolity and stupidity. Such qualities are also expressed with particular vividness in Poppel's naive and rude letter, which has been preserved to our own time, to Grand Prince Ivan III in 1490, which complains about his boiars and presents other shallow petitions. It is enough to read this missive to comprehend all the frivolity of its author and to endorse the opinion Russians had of it, namely, that Poppel "wrote his letter to our Sovereign in an unseemly manner," not as one should write to a great lord.

When Poppel was boasting in Moscow that he had discovered the Muscovite state for Europe, Moscow had already been opened to foreigners. Aristotle Fioravanti had erected there the Cathedral of the

Assumption, which was consecrated in 1479, and had built other churches, worked at a cannon foundry and minted coins. Other foreign specialists - Anton Friazin, Marco Ruffo, Pietro Solario and Alevisio - with Fioravanti's help had erected the towers and walls of the Kremlin. Construction of the stone buildings of the palace of the Kremlin had begun. Embassy after embassy had been sent to Italy to recruit technicians and masters of every "craft." At Russia's invitation, and even without invitation, Italians, Greeks and Germans came to serve in Moscow (such as "Albert, the German from Lübeck"). For all of them the road to Russia ran through that same Germany which had supposedly learned of Russia only from Poppel.

Some twenty years before Poppel's discoveries the Muscovite government was already conducting diplomatic relations with Italian courts, and the marriage alliance between Ivan III and the Greek princess, Sophia Paleologos, who resided at the Papal court, was being contemplated.[2] With the arrival of Princess Sophia and her suite in Moscow in 1472 a solid beginning was laid for Moscow's foreign colony, from which would come many of the Grand Prince's diplomats. One of these, Marco Ruffo, brought from Persia to Moscow the Venetian diplomat, Contarini, who had almost perished during his embassy to Persia.[3] Having reached Moscow (in 1476, ten years before Poppel), Contarini found there many Italians and Greeks and became closely acquainted with all of them. It proved possible for him to dispatch a messenger from Moscow to Venice for money, and he peacefully awaited his return to Moscow, passing there the entire fall and part of the winter of 1476. Observing Muscovite life, Contarini learned that "during the winter many merchants from Germany and Poland come together in Moscow to purchase various furs." At the beginning of 1477, earlier than he had expected, Contarini was released from Moscow in an unofficial manner, without an escort, and with only one *pristav (un huomo del signore),* and returned to his homeland through Lithuania, Poland and Germany, along the same well-worn route that the Polish and German merchants traveled to Moscow. En route he encountered his messenger in Jena, who brought him the money from Italy and accompanied him safely to Venice.

All these petty details clearly attest that by the close of the fifteenth century contacts between Moscow's court and market had already been secured with the West, and that Russia had no need to be "discovered" by wandering knights. It is true that these relations were limited to the demands of politics and commerce and had not yet grown into a common cultural bond. But for such contacts the soil had not been prepared even two centuries later.

II The Russian Question in Europe in the Middle of the Sixteenth Century. Schlitte and the System of Blockading Russia's Borders

If we grasp the idea that beginning with the fifteenth century Russia was acquainted with foreigners, communicated with European governments, admitted foreign merchants to her markets in Novgorod and Moscow and accepted foreign master craftsmen and technicians into her service, then we will not be surprised by the role assumed by the well-known adventurer of the mid-sixteenth century, Hans Schlitte. He visited Moscow during the years of the adolescence and youth of Ivan the Terrible, engaged in commercial activities there, learned the Russian language and, like many foreigners of the time, became an agent of the Muscovite government in its relations with the West. He was commissioned to recruit abroad all types of knowledgeable people and to bring them to Moscow.

Schlitte carried on this work in Germany and surrounded it with unusual attributes. He presented himself to the German Emperor, Charles V, as an envoy with a diplomatic mission from the Muscovite sovereign. In the name of Ivan the Terrible he proposed to Charles V that negotiations be initiated concerning the reunion of the Orthodox and Catholic churches. To be sure, in the instructions given him by Ivan the Terrible there is no mention of the reunion of the churches, but only the request that master craftsmen and learned men be allowed to pass into Russia. But for Schlitte it was important to impart to the matter precisely this tint of a religious nature. There is no need to consider him a visionary or dreamer; he had, it seems, a purely practical assessment of the personal qualities of Charles V and of the circumstances of that political moment. Schlitte was presented to the Catholic Emperor at Augsburg in the days when Charles had achieved a great victory over the Protestant princes of Germany. Being himself from Goslar, a Protestant town, Schlitte had to justify his orthodoxy to Charles were his mission to succeed. This he did very adroitly, suggesting to the Catholic monarch the possibility that he could triumph not only over the Protestants of Germany, but over Orthodoxy in Russia as well.

This flattery succeeded. The Emperor gave Schlitte permission to recruit the people he needed, provided that none of them went over to the Turks, the Tatars or to other non-Christian lands. Schlitte recruited 123 men, according to contemporary reports - "doctors, specialists and other learned men, bell-makers, miners and goldsmiths, architects, lapidaries, well-diggers, papermakers, surgeons, printers and other similar artisans." All were conveyed to Lübeck for subsequent passage to Russia, but here they were detained. Schlitte himself was even arrested, supposedly for having defaulted on the payment of a debt to the city of Lübeck, and was imprisoned. And while the matter of freeing him was being discussed, the people he had assembled dispersed. Thus the enterprise collapsed.

The cause of this, of course, was not Schlitte's indebtedness. It had quickly become known that master craftsmen and learned men were being recruited in Germany for service in Moscow. The leading circles of the Hanse, who were well acquainted with affairs in Russia, did not believe that Moscow had agreed to the reunion of the churches and considered all the possible consequences of free exchange of people between Russia and the West. Official letters were sent from Reval to Lübeck, the center of the Hanseatic League, asking that Schlitte not be allowed to go on to Moscow, in order to avoid the terrible misfortunes that would befall not only Livonia but the German nation as well, should the Russians master the military art and general technology of the West.

This fear of Russia gripped not only the military leaders of Reval, but Russia's other neighbors as well. When, having fled from Lübeck, Schlitte renewed his intrigue in favor of Moscow not only in Germany but in Rome as well, still playing on the same idea of religious reunion, the Polish government also opposed him. In 1553 it sent embassies to explain to the Emperor and the Pope the utter delusion of hopes for rapprochement with Russia. With complete justice the Poles pointed to the irreconcilable attitude of Russians toward the Pope and Catholicism and to the impossibility of alliance with Russia against the Turks. Like the members of the Hanse, the Poles feared the military strengthening of Russia and disclosed to the Pope the dangers that would threaten Europe, should the grand prince be excessively strengthened. Thus, thanks to Schlitte's intrigues, there arose in Europe for the first time the problem of the "Russian peril" and the necessity of conducting a policy of isolation and repression vis-a-vis Moscow.

Both the Emperor and the Pope pricked up their ears and responded with either evasion or direct refusal to all proposals of reunion or rapprochement, such as those falsely submitted in Ivan the Terrible's name by Schlitte. The Hanse and the Livonian towns firmly adopted the practice of passing across the border of Russia neither the people who could "civilize" Moscow nor goods that could increase the military might of the Muscovite sovereign. Moscow protested this policy of the Livonian authorities. In 1551 she even threatened war if they hindered Russian trade on their borders or detained foreigners coming to Moscow. Under such circumstances it remained for the Russians to obtain the needed technicians by all methods outside of open and official paths, and evidently they considered the most convenient indirect route to be Denmark, under whose flag it was possible to transport with less risk the necessary people and cargoes. A curious case in this regard occurred when Russia obtained a needed specialist from Denmark. During the war with Lithuania in 1535 Moscow first learned to assault a fortress by means of sapping and mines. That very year Lithuanian troops took from Russia the town of Starodub by "undermining the city with a cave." The Russian garrison at Starodub perished because "they did not recognize the slyness of undermining, for hitherto undermining had not been seen in our country." Moscow resolved to adopt and master "the craft of undermining" and by the time of the capture of Kazan (1552) already had in her army "a cunning German, skilled in destroying cities," who also had "students" who helped their German teacher undermine Kazan. From the name of this teacher, Rasmussen (the Russians pronounced it Razmysl), we can conclude that he was a Dane, obtained by Moscow from Denmark.

This, of course, is not the sole case of this sort of relations with Denmark. We know, for example, that at the beginning of 1553 Ivan the Terrible approached the Danish king, Christian III, with the request that a certain Arnd and "Caesar's people" be allowed to come to him in Moscow. Under the conditions of that moment, the "Caesar's people" could enter Moscow neither through Livonia nor through Lithuania; there remained for them the route through Denmark.

III The Northern Water Route to Russia: The English and Dutch in Moscow

Thus the problem of relations between Russia and the West was aggravated in the 1550's. Having been transferred to the realm of politics, it was settled unfavorably for Russia. But during these very years Russian life witnessed an event which at first appeared to be accidental, but which was in reality closely connected with the general development of international life in the West. This event was the arrival at the mouth of the Northern Dvina in 1553 of an English ship, the "Edward Bonaventure." One hundred and sixty tons in weight, this ship belonged to an expedition that had been outfitted by a company or society of English merchants to explore the water route to China ("Cathay") and India through the northern seas. This route they failed to find. Two of their three ships remained frozen in ice with all hands on the Russian coast of the Arctic Ocean. The third reached not India, but the Russian monastery of St. Nicholas of Karelia in the southern part of the mouth of the river Dvina. The date was August 24. The captain of the ship, Richard Chancellor, traveled by sea to the main Russian settlement on the Dvina, the town of Kholmogory. From there word was sent to Moscow of the appearance of English "German"[4] traders, and from Moscow came the order to send them to the capital. For the winter Chancellor and his *gosti,* that is, merchants and other fellow travelers, were dispatched to Moscow, while his ship and crew were sheltered in the Unskaia Inlet, which cuts deeply into the mainland.

The English appeared in Moscow just as the Russian people were suffering the indignity of having their western border closed. This event brought hope for a satisfactory escape from this crisis. Instead of using the harbors of the Baltic and the border at Smolensk, the Muscovite state could import the people and goods it needed through "God's road - the ocean sea," through the mouth of the Dvina. Besides, the Russians realized that the English ships could bring goods directly from European harbors to Russia without transfers en route, as they were obliged to do in the Baltic.

Up to that time the Russian people had used the White Sea only rarely, in dealing with Denmark. From the White Sea they sailed along the coast of Murmansk to Trondheim in Norway, or even to Bergen, and from there went overland to Copenhagen. But this route was complicated and awkward. It could be used only in exceptional cases and could not be used at all for trade or the transport of goods. With the appearance of the Englishmen, however, the White Sea water route to the English harbors became the most convenient one, completely independent of hostile neighbors. It created the possibility of direct and regular relations with the West precisely at the moment that these relations had been forcibly severed along all the routes that previously had been operative. The happiness and cordiality with which the English merchants were greeted in Moscow are therefore understandable, as is the generosity with which the Muscovite government bestowed kindness and lavished privileges upon these long desired newcomers.

In the course of a few years the English consolidated their commercial link with Russia. At the Monastery of St. Nicholas of Karelia on the island of Yagra at the mouth of the Dvina they built their own dock and settlement. This island, where many wild, red roses grew, was named "Rose Island." Here stood English homes and warehouses for goods. Here ships were unloaded. From here on light vessels, "plank boats" and "bait boats," English goods went to Kholmogory and Vologda. Here Russian goods were brought for shipment to England. Along the entire route from Kholmogory to

Moscow, in the main towns, the Englishmen were provided grounds for residences and there they erected homes and warehouses. They especially valued Vologda as the best place to store English goods, for "Vologda enjoyed an excellent position and traded with all the towns of the Muscovite state." There they built their own trading station, which was, according to the description of a contemporary, as spacious as a castle. In Moscow the English had a residence in the Kitaigorod on the Varvarka, near the church of Maxim the Confessor. During the fire of 1571, when the Crimean Tatars attacked Moscow, about thirty Englishmen, men, women and children of the local English colony, died of burns and suffocation.[5]

In addition to their commercial warehouses and residences the English attempted to establish factories to process Russian raw materials. As early as 1557 they began to build in Kholmogory a ropewalk operated by skilled workmen from London. Somewhat later the English were permitted to erect on the river Vychegda an iron-works to process the ore discovered there.

But undertakings of this sort played only a secondary role in the minds of the English entrepreneurs. Their primary attention was fixed on other matters. First, they wished to exploit the natural resources of the Russian North, especially its furs. Secondly, they attempted to establish contact with Asian markets via the Muscovite domain and to reach China and India. Both these objectives they pursued with unusual energy.

Within a short time the English explorers had become acquainted with the main routes of the Pomorie, the coasts eastward as well as westward from the Dvina. They succeeded in going from Kholmogory to the Solovki Islands in the White Sea, from there to the mouth of the river Vyg, along the Vyg to the portages near Povents, and from there via lakes Onega and Ladoga and the river Volkhov to Novgorod. From the other side they reached the river Pechora by land and sea and investigated both the passage by sea to the Pechora Inlet and the river routes via the Pinega, Mezen and Peza, as well as the winter routes between the major inhabited points from Kholmogory to Ust Tsilma and Pustozersk. They were particularly interested in Lampozhnia on the Mezen, a place where twice yearly the largest fair of the Russian

Sixteenth Century and Time of Troubles

North was held. There Russian merchants and natives brought from the Pechora and even the Ob (Mangazeia) all types of furs, deer hides and walrus tusks. There these wares were bought by traders from Kholmogory and were distributed throughout the Muscovite state. The Englishmen vigorously participated in this trade and brought to Lampozhnia their own cloth and metal wares to exchange for precious furs, which were sent to England.

While investigating this region they also explored the coasts and islands of the Arctic Ocean. The idea of reaching the Asian continent from the north continued to preoccupy the English, despite the failure of their first attempt in 1553, and they dispatched new expeditions in search of this route. Especially noteworthy were the surveys of the northern seas by Stephen Burrough, who during a single summer (1556) reached the Kola Inlet, then made his way to Kanin Nos, Yugoria, the island of Vaigacha and even Novaia Zemlia. But his hopes of reaching the mouths of the Ob River were unrealized, and he returned to winter at the mouth of the Northern Dvina. Of the many Englishmen who sailed the Arctic Ocean, Burrough was the most scientific and exact explorer. It was largely through his efforts that England acquired the material for a good map of the northern coasts of Russia.

It can be said that at the end of the sixteenth century the English had made the Russian North completely their own and for years at a time lived, traded and earned their living not only in such busy settlements as Kholmogory and Lampozhnia, but also in such distant and remote corners as Ust Tsilma and Pustozersk on the Pechora.

Their second objective, that of reaching Asia via Muscovy, the English pursued with no less energy. Here their pioneer was the remarkable traveler, Anthony Jenkinson, who has left us interesting notes about the Russia of his day. Prior to his appearance in Russia he had traveled much in Europe and had been in Turkey, Palestine and North Africa. In the winter of 1557-58 he came to Moscow and received permission from the Tsar to undertake a trip to the countries of Asia. In the spring he set sail along the Volga, with China his ultimate objective. From Astrakhan he sailed on a ship with Persian and Tatar merchants that crossed the Caspian Sea and landed on the Mangyshlak Peninsula. From there he reached Bukhara, not without great adventures. Jenkinson wintered in Bukhara and in the spring of 1559 intended to go on to China. But constant wars and acts of brigandage by nomads closed all routes to him and forced him to return to Moscow. But he did not stop at this first attempt. In 1561 he again came to Moscow from England and, with the Tsar's permission, set out for Persia. This time his route from Astrakhan went by way of Derbent and Shemaka. He stayed in Tavriz, met the Shah in Kazvin, wintered there and in the summer of 1563 safely returned to Moscow.

Observant and educated, Jenkinson was equally well suited for commercial, diplomatic and scientific work. His geographical observations and computations, his ethnographic descriptions, his information on commerce and his diplomatic negotiations were all of great benefit to the English government and to the commercial organizations with which he was associated. Historians and geographers alike consult Jenkinson's works as most useful for an appreciation of the countries he explored. Having won the favor of Ivan the Terrible, Jenkinson was able to secure from him broad privileges for English trade not only in Kholmogory and Moscow, but also in Kazan, Astrakhan, Narva and Dorpat. Most remarkable of all, he obtained for the English trading company to which he belonged the right to transport goods duty free to Persia, and to Bukhara and Samarkand in Central Asia.

After Jenkinson several other agents of the English trading company were dispatched along the Asian routes (Thomas Alcock, George Wren, Richard Chaney, Richard Johnson and Arthur Edwards). For the time being the Russian government encouraged all such enterprises by the Englishmen. Their trading companies were given the right of duty free trade throughout the Muscovite state. In certain cities they were allowed to build their trading stations, which enjoyed broad autonomy. Individual Englishmen were even permitted to settle and trade within the country, as long as their company did not object. Finally, the Russian government eagerly turned to England for the specialists it needed, and it received them.

But this state of affairs lasted only until ships of other nations followed the English to the northern Russian harbors. Then dissension arose between the English government and the Muscovite authorities.

England insisted that she maintain her rights not only of duty free trade, but of exclusive use of the water route to Russia. But the Russians refused to recognize that right, simply because they could not understand it. The English said that they "were the first to find the water route to Russia, with great losses and suffering," and therefore "no one should be allowed to come to Russia, except those who had lived and supported themselves there after the first voyage." As it is reproduced in Muscovite translation, the English letter on this matter advanced the claim to monopoly of trade and noted in general that "those who made the journey and found the harbor are held in great esteem in all lands." Russian diplomats answered these claims by noting that the commercial rights of the English within the Muscovite state had not at all diminished, that "their traders had enjoyed exemption from duty for many years and had made much profit," and that there had never been a time when the English were the only foreigners to come to Russia from abroad. During the years that they used the harbor at the mouths of the Dvina many other foreigners had used the port of Narva. Only after Muscovy lost Narva in 1581 were all foreigners in general directed to the Northern Dvina; and for this purpose the new town of Archangel was founded there in 1584.

There was truth in these explanations. The Russians proceeded from the assumption that "God's great road - the ocean sea" was open equally to all and that it was impossible to "close" or "appropriate" it. They knew that while the English had been trading on the Dvina in the 1560's, trade with the Dutch had begun in Pechenga and at Kola in the Murmansk region. And they understood that under existing circumstances preservation of the English monopoly in the North was unprofitable for the state and even unrealistic. They could hardly drive away from those harbors the non-English ships coming there to trade.

Thus the English had to live with the idea that the northern route to the Muscovite state had been opened for other nations as well. Especially bitter and harmful for the English in Russia became the rivalry of the Dutch, who at that time were rapidly striding toward predominance in world trade.

It is well known that the Dutch first appeared on the Arctic Ocean no earlier than the middle of the sixteenth century. It is said that the first Dutch ship visited Vardohüys on the northern coast of Norway in 1564. In 1565 the Dutch had reached Pechenga Bay and afterwards Kola Bay, near the village of Kola. In 1566 and 1567 two Dutchmen, Van Salingen and De Meyer, without any official permission, reached Moscow from Kola via Kandalaksha and Lake Onega, visited Novgorod and successfully returned home not only with profits but also with much valuable information. Thereafter the Dutch started visiting Kola regularly and began trading with the Russians. With the same energy as the English, they undertook the investigation of the northern coasts of the Muscovite state.

Among them were explorers who were in no way inferior to Jenkinson and Burrough. Van Salingen, who has been mentioned already, spent more than thirty years studying the Russian North, learned to speak Russian, struck up acquaintances with Russians who lived along the coast, served as a translator for the Danish government in its relations with Russia, compiled reports and notes on Russian affairs for the Danes and the Dutch, went to Moscow as an ambassador of the Danish king and, finally, drew up a geographical map of Scandinavia, Lapland and Finland. The Dutch and the Danes regarded him as their most useful informant on Russian affairs.

More remarkable still were the activities of a native of Brussels, Oliver Brunel. He came to Kola as a young man on one of the first Dutch ships and was sent from there to Kholmogory to learn the Russian language. Because of some denunciation or other he was arrested, sent deep into the interior of Russia and thrown into prison in Yaroslavl. According to the custom of the time, any foreign prisoner taken in war could be freed from prison on bail to work in private business. Brunel was apparently numbered among such prisoners and was bailed out of prison by the famous Stroganovs, who took him into their service.[6] He became a commercial agent for them and more than once transported their wares and furs abroad for sale in Antwerp and Paris. This was in the 1570's. Later the Stroganovs sent him to the eastern lands of Russia. Twice he traveled to Siberia, to the mouths of the river Ob and went down to the sea along the Pechora. Thus he became well acquainted with the conditions of sailing along the Siberian coasts.

Sixteenth Century and Time of Troubles

In 1581 Brunel organized an extremely interesting expedition. In the name of the Stroganovs he went to Holland, in order to invite experienced sailors to man two ships built by the Stroganovs. With these sailors Brunel was to skirt Siberia and reach China. But the voyage, which began in 1584, was unsuccessful because of ice, and shortly thereafter Brunel deserted the Stroganovs and joined the service of the King of Denmark.

His precise and valuable observations were of great service to his countrymen's relations with Russia. It is supposedly through his initiative that the Dutch succeeded in finding the route to the mouths of the Northern Dvina. Under his guidance Jan van de Walle in 1577 or 1578 brought the first Dutch ship to the Monastery of St. Nicholas. Thereafter it was easy for other Dutch ships to find the same route. The Dutch, however, did not become neighbors of the English at St. Nicholas. They entered the Dvina through its Pudozhem Mouth, about ten miles further on, and there they built their first dock. Later, in 1582, they advanced still higher up the river to the Monastery of Archangel, where the Muscovite government had begun to build a "town" (that is, a fortress), and under the walls of this town warehouses were erected.

This new town of Archangel rapidly grew in importance as an organized landing harbor, and in 1585 the Tsar decreed that in the future foreigners should bring their ships only to Archangel and that they should relocate their homes and warehouses - the English from Rose Island and the Dutch from the Pudozhem Mouth. From that time onward Archangel became the main, even the sole, Russian port in the North, for simultaneously with its construction the government closed to foreigners the harbors of Kola and Pechenga on the Murmansk coast and allowed them to trade there only in cod, halibut and whale blubber.

With the building of the town of Archangel Russian trade privileges became equitable for all nations. It is true that the English company retained its former privilege of duty free trade and therein had no competitor. But the import of goods to the harbor, the distribution of goods throughout the Russian towns, the construction of trading centers in the most important locations throughout the country, and the freedom of movement of commercial agents, were all administered equitably for English and Dutch alike. Both were completely free to demonstrate their business skills, and it must be said that the Dutch very soon proved themselves dangerous rivals. The first Dutch trader to reach Archangel, Jan van de Walle (who was known in Moscow as Ivan Deval Beloborod), had already won the special affection of Ivan the Terrible for having brought him "luxurious" and especially valuable goods, "while the English *gosti* never brought such goods." As time passed the rivalry of the Dutch became more vigorous and they became more firmly settled in Moscow itself and in other towns, until they finally achieved clear superiority over the English. The entire seventeenth century is a time of uninterrupted successes by the Dutch in the Muscovite state.

IV The Livonian War and the War Prisoners. The "Sailing to Narva"

In this manner Moscow in her relations with Western Europe achieved emancipation from her immediate western neighbors. The English and the Dutch, who were readily available and dependent upon no one, replaced the Italians and the "foreigners from Caesar's lands" (that is, the Germans), whom the government of Livonia, the Polish-Lithuanian Commonwealth *[Rech Pospolita]* and the Hanseatic towns had refused to allow into Russia. But this does not mean that there was no influx of people across Russia's western border. On the contrary, this influx increased during the second half of the sixteenth century, thanks to the Livonian War waged by Ivan the Terrible.

At the beginning of 1558 the final rift occurred between Russia and Livonia. Russian troops invaded Estland and Livland, devastated the country and brought from there to Russia a large number of prisoners who were enslaved. Some of them passed into the hands of private individuals, who either sold them on the side or attached them to their personal estates as "bondmen." The great majority of them were common folk of Estonian or Latvian origin, who formed a crude work force. Prisoners of higher calibre - persons who had belonged to the

Sixteenth Century and Time of Troubles 15

German upper classes of Livonia or who, to use our own expression, were skilled - usually were made state or "sovereign's prisoners." These were at the disposal of the state, in its own service, and were distributed throughout the country. In the eastern regions of the state, for example, such prisoners formed the town garrisons.

Interesting information concerning the fate of these prisoners circulated at that time in Germany. In one of the memoranda composed for the Holy Roman Emperor concerning the Baltic question, there is a positive indication that the Tsar of Moscow treated German prisoners with kindness and that some 9,000 Livonian prisoners had not been sold into slavery, as had been rumored, but were settled in various towns. Russian documents also provide evidence of this way of using prisoners. For the same time to which the German note refers (the 1560's), we have also Russian data on the small fortified town of Laishev on the Kama River. This town was located on and commanded the fords across the lower course of the Kama and defended Kazan against incursions by Siberian tribesmen. In its garrison were 150 "captured inhabitants of the settlement," who were allotted a good deal of "prisoners' plowing land" in the farming tracts of "good land." These prisoners, who were "Germans" and "Lithuanians," remained settled in the towns of the Volga even after the Livonian War. They apparently felt at home on the "good land" and did not long for their former way of life. For at least forty years after their settlement on the Volga the "Lithuanians" and "Germans" continued to serve in the garrisons of the Kama region.

Common soldiers taken in battle by the Russians suffered the fate of simple military service. The more eminent of the prisoners fared better, finding even in Moscow positions that were commensurate with their knowledge and ability. The clearest example of how this sort of prisoner was able to make a career for himself is that of the noblemen from Livland, Johann Taube and Elert Kruse. They belonged to the Livonian aristocracy, participated in the struggle with Muscovy and were taken prisoner by Ivan the Terrible. They won the favor and trust of the Tsar by promising to serve him and to help him subdue Livonia. He made them his diplomatic agents and through their services he conducted negotiations with the Livonian authorities and the Danish government. They were also charged with military duties. But after an assault that they had organized against Dorpat ended in failure, they feared disfavor and decided to betray Ivan the Terrible by fleeing to Lithuania and to Hetman Chodkiewicz, to whom they dedicated their famous memoir or "missive" on the "unprecedented tyranny" of Ivan the Terrible.

They had served Russia for at least six years before they forsook it, and these were the years (1566-72) of the most intense terror of the *oprichnina*,[7] which, however, had not caused them the least harm. There is evidence that Kruse had enjoyed the special favor of the Tsar. Ivan restored his family to him, gave him a stone house and land, fixed a salary in money on him, supplied him in kind from the tsarist court and, above all else, promised to entrust to him only "honorable matters." Taube had also received from the Tsar a large *pomestie* estate in Riazan, lands in the Bishopric of Dorpat, a substantial salary in money and other gifts. The prosperity of these "episcopal advisers" from Dorpat was well known in Germany.

It was also known in Germany that still greater favor than that won by Taube and Kruse was enjoyed in Moscow by Adrian Kalb and Caspar von Eberfeld, who were also of Dorpat. About Eberfeld there was even the rumor that the Tsar trusted him so much that he was continually being summoned to the *boiar duma* and more than once had dared to argue with the Tsar about the superiority of the Protestant faith. Also listed among the prisoners who were held in affection and respect in Moscow was Pastor Wettermann of Dorpat, whom the Tsar allowed to see and read the Greek, Latin and other foreign language books in his library.

We could name many other Livonians who lived in the service and at the expense of the Russian government and who suffered neither persecution nor particular want during their captivity. Nor could they have been few in numbers, for Ivan the Terrible at times undertook a so-called "deportation" in the countries he conquered, that is, a massive resettlement of the inhabitants of a subdued town into the interior of the Muscovite state. He did this to Dorpat in 1565, when he ordered removed from the town its "German mayors, city commissioners and councilmen for transfer to Vladimir, Kostroma, Nizhnii Novgorod and

Uglich." The Tsar explained this measure by saying that the Germans of Dorpat "were in communication with the Grand Master of Livonia and told him to come to their town with many men." Thus during the very first years of the Livonian War, Moscow and other Russian towns saw Livonian prisoners in quite large numbers.

But prisoners were not the sole source from which a foreign element entered the Russian land at that time across its western borders. During the very first months of the war, in May of 1558, Muscovite troops captured Narva and Russia thereby obtained one of the finest harbors on the eastern coasts of the Baltic. The Muscovite government understood its importance very well. In the words of G. V. Forsten, who has studied the Baltic question, Narva was Ivan the Terrible's favorite offspring. The Russians quickly repaired the town, which had suffered from fire and assault, and built a bridge across the Narova River, thereby connecting Narva with Ivangorod. Russian commanders helped the neighboring inhabitants to recover from the destruction and issued them grain, horses and cattle. The inhabitants of Narva received permission "to live in their own place." Those who had been captured during the assault were released from captivity. All prisoners from Narva "who had not yet been sold in other lands" were ordered to be sought out and returned to the city. The city was given the right of free and duty free trade with the Muscovite state and was granted the opportunity to trade and to maintain relations with other countries. All kinds of steps were taken to attract foreigners to the harbor of Narva, and they were promised personal security and commercial privileges of every kind. Narva assumed the role formerly played by Novgorod, which previously had been the main center of trade between Russia and the foreign markets of the Baltic.

The appearance of the Russians in Narva and their opening of its harbor to free trade made a great impression upon interested circles in Germany and the Scandinavian states. Until that moment Russo-Hanseatic trade had been in the hands of the Livonian towns, especially Reval, which had opposed in every way possible the development of trade between Vyborg and Narva and the merchants of Muscovy. Now Reval began to fight the "Narva sailing" with a mailed fist, forcibly detaining ships going to Narva and seeking supporters and allies among neighboring states. Hence Reval's gravitation toward Sweden, which in the end gave the Swedes all of Estland.

By contrast, the opening of the harbor at Narva caused great happiness in Lübeck and in the western Hanseatic towns generally. These towns willingly sent to Narva ships that bypassed Reval and went straight to their destination, thereby avoiding delays and reloading in Reval and escaping the unnecessary expense connected therewith. Danish ships sailed to Narva in the same manner, despite the vicissitudes that occurred in the political relations of Denmark and Russia. Dutch and English merchants who did not belong to the English company that had the trading monopoly at the mouths of the Northern Dvina also learned of the free trade in the Muscovite port. Even the Swedish king, Eric XIV, who supported Reval in its struggle against Narva, looked through his fingers at Swedish and Finnish subjects who went to Narva and profitably brought back goods needed by the Swedes. In brief, the "Narva sailing" immediately achieved very great significance, for it opened to Europe a new route for receiving Russian raw materials, which were, as contemporaries said, an inexhaustible source of blessings.

Narva became a lively port, and a bitter struggle began to boil up along its approaches. Enemies and defenders of the "Narva sailing" acted forcefully, kept pirate ships at sea and seized their enemies and competitors. In this respect Russia did not lag behind the others; and she had on the Baltic her own privateers to defend trading ships going to Narva. These were commanded by the German captain, Carsten Rode. He seized all whom he considered enemies of the Tsar or personal enemies and acted the brigand as much as other privateers, which in the end landed him in a Danish prison. Yet despite all the dangers of navigation and the risk of suffering losses en route to the new Russian market, Narva attracted many traders and became, like the mouth of the Northern Dvina, a lively place of commercial exchange between Central Europe and Russia as long as Moscow was its master, that is, until 1581.

V Ivan the Terrible and Foreigners

And so from the 1550's there was a great influx of western Europeans into the Muscovite state. The English were in the Pomorie, in Vologda, Yaroslavl and in Moscow itself. They were also on the routes to Central Asia. They were in Narva and Novgorod too. The Dutch were in the harbors of Murmansk, at the Northern Dvina and followed the English along the entire route from Kholmogory to Moscow. They too were in Narva and Novgorod as well. There were the "Germans" from Livonia, the prisoners who were settled throughout the entire state and who lived in their own communities, with their own pastors and places of worship. There were merchants from Germany and Livonia, who had reached Russian markets through Narva and other routes open to them despite the war. All these people were a novelty to Russia and her interior regions. They could not help but influence the Russian people, especially the court and commercial circles.

Ivan the Terrible himself, with his keen mind and nervous sensitivity, fell under the charm of these interesting newcomers. There are valuable indications of this in the writings of the Englishmen who were in Moscow during Ivan the Terrible's reign. The Tsar did not merely display gracious kindness to them in matters of etiquette; he also privately contacted English diplomats and commercial agents. Thus when he met Jenkinson in the Kremlin on the day of the blessing of the waters (January 6, 1558),[8] the Tsar recognized him, even though Jenkinson was wearing Russian dress, engaged him in conversation and personally invited him to dinner. When Jenkinson returned to Moscow from Bukhara a year and a half later, the Tsar discussed with him over dinner the countries he had seen. During frequent conversations with the Englishman Horsey,[9] the Tsar questioned him about the military fleet of England, then ordered the *diak,* Elizar Vyluzgin, to record the information Horsey had related. If we are to believe Horsey, on the very morning of the Tsar's death he saw Ivan in his domestic surroundings, in the company of his closest courtiers. In his presence Ivan the Terrible examined the precious stones in his casket, with no presentiment of his death.

An official record for the end of 1583 relates the conversation Ivan had with the English ambassador, Bowes, which was more than an exchange of ideas concerning business. The Tsar boasted to the ambassador of the things sold him by the Dutch merchant, Van de Walle (known in Moscow as Ivan Beloborod). "The Tsar took from his hand and showed the ambassador a ring" and showed him the "large emerald that he used as a button on his cowl," and said that "the English *gosti* never sold such goods." The English ambassador kissed the ring with praise and highly complimented the button on his cowl (that is, the clasp on the Tsar's cap). This petty detail illustrates the degree of informality with which the Tsar treated foreigners and his disposition toward them. It is interesting that when Ivan the Terrible died, his *diak,* Andrei Shchelkalov, ordered that Bowes be told the news with the words, "your English Tsar has died." He was not ashamed to censure with this unwarranted gibe what he considered to be the Tsar's disposition toward the English.

But Shchelkalov was not alone in his displeasure with Ivan the Terrible's attitude toward foreigners. When Elisaeus Bomel, the astrologer and physician who had come from England, won the Tsar's favor, it occasioned a general scandal in 1570. Bomel proved to be a great intriguer and a crafty fox. It is said that he circumvented Ivan by insinuating himself into his trust, told his fortune as an astrologer and served him by making potions used to poison those who had fallen into disfavor. He marked for death many boiars. It was believed that he suggested to Ivan the idea of marrying Queen Elizabeth of England.[10] His influence upon Ivan was considered to be extraordinary, and there was rejoicing when in 1580 he himself was charged with treason and was tortured to death.

Bomel's fame was so widespread and the account of his power so bruited about that even a remote provincial chronicle of the time told of him in epic tones. According to this chronicle, which was hostile to Moscow, the Germans and Lithuanians had cunningly sent to Ivan the Terrible "a foreigner, a fierce sorcerer named Elisei, who was close to and favored by the Tsar and caused the Tsar to fear him, and led the Tsar into error. He led the Tsar away from the faith, of course, and caused him to become vicious toward the Russian people and to love foreigners." The enemies of Ivan the Terrible "had learned through their own sorcery that in the end he would destroy them, and for this reason they sent such a wicked heretic to him." And they had reckoned correctly. The heretic Bomel "stirred up many, many boiars and princes to kill the Tsar, then convinced the Tsar that his life was in danger and that he should flee to England and marry there, and beat down the boiars who remained." Bomel's evil influence was, according to the chronicle, ended by these same boiars, who finally "handed him over to death." Such representations of events in Moscow appeared in districts far from the capital.

One Muscovite *diak* and writer of the period, Ivan Timofeev, judged the matter more rationally, though also more guardedly. He briefly says that Ivan the Terrible killed his nobles or banished them to foreign lands and in their place "loved" foreigners. The foreigners alone he enriched with generous gifts, while some of them he even made his advisers. There were also some who were close to him because of their "slyness in doctoring" (a reference to Bomel). But these brought harm, and not health, to his soul, as well as the "hatred of his people." Timofeev is astonished that the Tsar, "with so little wisdom," was overcome not by his enemies, but by "the weakness of his own conscience" and placed his own head "in the viper's mouth." "Alas," he exclaims, "every barbarian in our state had him in his grasp." They did with him whatever they wished! This was the impression Ivan the Terrible made upon people who saw with their own eyes life in Moscow and conditions at court during his time. It is apparent that the importance of foreigners in Moscow had so increased at the time of Ivan the Terrible that it became the problem of the day for Russians and gave them grounds for charging the Tsar with defection from ancient custom to the side of the foreign newcomers.

Foreigners themselves have recorded with special emphasis the freedom with which Ivan the Terrible trespassed the limits of etiquette and business in dealing with them. Even if we cannot believe Horsey, who may have exaggerated his closeness to the Tsar out of vanity, we must believe, for example, the English ambassador Thomas Randolph and his most interesting account of a meeting at night with Ivan the Terrible in February, 1569. The Tsar desired to speak with him secretly and summoned him late at night, several days after an open audience with him, through a close and trusted boiar. "The place for the meeting was far off," Randolph says, "and the night was cold; and I, having changed my apparel into such as the Russes do wear, found great incommodity thereby. Having talked with him above three hours, towards morning I was dismissed and so came home to my lodging." At this unusual meeting political and commercial problems were discussed and resolved without regard for the customary official forms. These forms were observed only later, several weeks after the nocturnal meeting.

Foreigners have also recorded the freedom with which Ivan the Terrible addressed them in conversations on religious themes. In the 1560's there was talk in Lübeck of how Ivan loved to touch upon questions of the church with Livonian prisoners, how he argued the differences between Orthodoxy and Catholicism and how he seemed to be considering reunion of the churches. It was pointed out how the prisoner from Dorpat, Eberfeld, had freely disclosed to the Tsar the advantages of the Protestant confession and how the pastor from Dorpat, Wettermann, had been allowed into Ivan's own library, in order to become acquainted with its theological works, and how Ivan with perfect tolerance allowed the holding of Protestant services and permitted the building of a church for captured Germans. Reports of this type are supported by documents that allow no doubts.

Also well known is the episode of the theologian, Jan Rokyta, who belonged to the sect of the "Moravian Brethren." With other members of that sect he left the Czech lands for Poland and from there came to Moscow in 1570 in the retinue of a Lithuanian embassy to Ivan the Terrible. When he was presented to Ivan, he was rewarded with a long conversation with him "concerning faith" and, of course, disagreed with the Orthodox Tsar in his beliefs. Both discussants then committed their argument to paper. Rokyta recorded his debate with the Tsar in Polish, and this work was published in a Latin translation in 1582. The comments of the Tsar remained in manuscript form until the nineteenth century and circulated among Russian and western European writers. It is difficult to say whether Ivan the Terrible himself composed them, or whether they were done by someone else at his direction. But that this debate with the pastor took place is

Sixteenth Century and Time of Troubles 23

indisputable, as is the fact that Rokyta was given the opportunity to express freely before the Tsar his own sectarian doctrine.

But Ivan the Terrible did not always maintain this manner of religious tolerance. There is the tale of how another pastor suffered from a conversation with the Tsar for having compared Luther with the apostle Paul at the wrong moment. The Tsar, it seems, struck him on the head with his staff and told him to "go to the devil with your Luther." It can be assumed that Ivan's manifestations of tolerance and his kind attentions to those of other faiths were dictated not so much by his personal interest in differences between the churches as by considerations of a practical nature.

It is, of course, unthinkable that the Tsar wavered in his Russian Orthodoxy even for a moment. As regards Protestant teachings, which were new to the Tsar, inasmuch as they had arisen only during his time and were directed against Catholicism (even as Orthodoxy itself was directed against Catholicism), Ivan was motivated by interest in and a lively desire to learn of this new religious movement. But as far as the "Roman faith" was concerned, discussion of it was allowed by the Tsar only under special circumstances.

A case in point is that of the well known Papal ambassador, Antonio Possevino. He had been sent to Moscow to mediate between Ivan the Terrible and King Stefan Bathory of Poland and had been instructed to try in every way possible to reunite the churches and bend Moscow to the views of the Papal throne. From the very first moment that Possevino appeared on Russian soil, Ivan the Terrible had misgivings about raising the question of faith. The *pristav* who was dispatched to meet Possevino on the border in July, 1581 had been ordered in advance to shun any conversation on matters of faith. In case Possevino should "try to argue and speak of the Greek and Roman faith, Zaleshin (the *pristav*) was to refuse to read or speak of anything concerning the faith, under the pretext that he was not a learned man."

When Possevino arrived in Moscow the Tsar also postponed discussion of theological matters in every way possible, introducing first and foremost the political matters about which Possevino had come. He sent Possevino to Bathory to achieve peace and promised that once peace was secured, "then we shall let you know about faith." But when a truce was signed and Possevino reappeared in Moscow (in February, 1582), Ivan was not inclined to engage him in theological discussions. Possevino assumed that his primary task was elucidation of the possibility of religious union between Moscow and Rome and therefore insisted that the Tsar listen to his words about union at least once ("to listen at least once to Antonio in private," as it was said in the notes that Possevino presented to the boiars). Ivan declined to listen to the Jesuit in private, without witnesses, yet he did not think it proper to deny him completely the conversation he wished. The conversation took place in the presence of a few witnesses and was officially recorded by Russian *diaki.* In this record the Tsar's behavior is depicted with complete exactness. He refused to speak of faith, he said, for two reasons. First, he "had not been blessed and consecrated" for this by the Orthodox clergy. Secondly, he was afraid of disturbing political accord through a theological argument. But "the ambassador Antonio was insistent" and "said to the sovereign with annoyance that this would give rise to no argument and that he greatly desired to speak of faith with the sovereign." Yielding to Possevino's insistence, Ivan did not terminate the discussion but led him to talk of trifles, explaining frankly that "we do not wish to speak with you of the great matters of the faith, lest you become vexed."

He intentionally began with an insignificant question: why did Possevino shave his beard, although that was "not allowed?" "In the Roman faith you cut the beard of the Pope, but tell us from whom and from what teaching you accept this."[11] When Possevino ended this derisive topic by declaring that "he does not cut or shave his beard," Ivan went on to another subject, equally insignificant, of how people bow to the ground before the Pope, and of how "on the Pope's boot there is a cross, and on the cross the crucifixion." In Ivan's opinion, "one should not kiss the Pope's foot," nor should "one wear a cross lower than one's belt, for it is unseemly to wear anything that is holy lower than one's belt." Yet the Pope "out of pride has established this (indecent) ceremony." Possevino explained why such honor is rendered the Pope and, as a proof that bowing to the ground was not an honor reserved for the Pope alone, "Antonio bowed at the feet of the sovereign." But Ivan the Terrible was not touched. He observed that in general "it is unseemly to fall at people's feet," and that the Pope should not be haughty but should "show an example of humility." He added that "any Pope who does not know how to live according to the teaching of Christ and the tradition of the Apostles is not a pastor, but a wolf." From this Possevino was convinced that the discussion would be of no benefit "and stopped speaking, saying that if you call the Pope a wolf, you are calling me a snake." But Ivan then observed, "I have already told you that if we speak of faith we shall not escape words of dissension." He graciously dismissed the Jesuit, patted him with his hand and gave it to him to kiss.[12]

We cannot deny that the Tsar was adroit in polemics. By intentionally keeping to "insignificant affairs" and not permitting "words of great matters concerning the faith," he virtually eluded completely an exchange of ideas about reunion and left the Jesuit, and through him also Pope Gregory XIII, without satisfaction. Least of all can naivety and simple-mindedness be seen in the Tsar's behavior. One can only argue a bit about which predominated in him: calculating slyness or the inclination, which was peculiar to Ivan the Terrible, of jesting and mockery. Possevino, it seems, saw the latter. In subsequent conversations with Ivan he merely listened to the Tsar and refrained from speech, though he did not conceal his displeasure.

VI Contact Between the Russian People and Foreigners. The Foreign Settlement in Moscow

Such were the relations of the Tsar of Russia with foreigners. From everything that has been reported above, it is clear that he did not shun them, that he was accustomed to them and that he was in constant contact with them and often showed them favor and kindness. In the opinion of Russians, this kindness occasionally went beyond bounds. They were astonished and indignant that the Tsar allowed himself to become so closely acquainted with these "barbarians." They recalled Timofeev's words that "every barbarian in our state had him in his grasp."

Unfortunately, we have almost no material to judge how deep and widespread was the influence of foreigners upon the various classes of the Russian population. Of course, the court and officials that surrounded Ivan the Terrible became as accustomed as he to contacts with representatives of European governments and business organizations. Through diplomatic relations ("reponsibilities," as they were termed in those days) with them in Moscow and through journeys to foreign courts new knowledge and customs were gained and new types of people emerged.

One of these new men was Feodor Pisemsky, a professional diplomat in the days of Ivan the Terrible. He was of the nobility of Galich, was elevated to the Muscovite nobility in 1550, participated in the subjugation of Astrakhan, went more than once on embassies to the Crimea and Poland, took part in negotiations with Possevino, attended a conference with Swedish diplomatic agents in 1590 and, finally, directed an embassy from Ivan the Terrible to Queen Elizabeth of England in 1582. He happened to be captured by the Livonians while he was still quite young, and amazed them by his knowledge and intelligence. According to their testimony, he had mastered the Latin, Greek, Polish and Russian languages, spoke some French and German, and was very intelligent and quick. Inasmuch as there is no basis for believing that Pisemsky had spent his youth abroad, we must suppose that his learning was acquired in Moscow, and at an early time - the 1550's (he was captured in 1559). Apparently Pisemsky had been prepared from his youth for the diplomatic service, where he found his historical role.

Others among his contemporaries were educated differently. In the writings of Kurbsky there is a very interesting, albeit somewhat inconsistent, account of two members of the Lykov family who were executed by Ivan the Terrible. Kurbsky briefly sets before the reader the biographies of the Lykovs. One of them, Mikhail Matveevich Lykov, was captured in his childhood by "old King Sigismund." His father, Matvei Lykov, perished when Sigismund Augustus took Radogoshch in 1534, but his family survived and was maintained very well in Poland at the king's residence. The king commanded "not only that they be fed in his own royal chambers, but ordered his own doctor (that is, a scholar) to teach them the knowledge enjoyed by the gentry, as well as the Roman language." In 1542 Russian ambassadors in Cracow "entreated the king to return them to their fatherland," and two of the Lykov brothers, Ivan and Mikhail, returned to the Muscovite state and served a fatherland that was, in Kurbsky's expression, "ungrateful to and unworthy of its learned men."

Kurbsky mentions the Lykovs in his *History of the Great Prince of Moscow* because, according to his testimony, Mikhail was executed by Ivan the Terrible. Also put to death with him was his "close kinsman," whose name Kurbsky does not provide, but who is even more interesting for our purposes than the other Lykovs. According to Kurbsky's description, he was "a very fine youth." He "was sent across the sea for learning to Germany, and there became very familiar with the German spoken and written language. He remained there and studied for quite a few years and traveled throughout all of Germany, then was returned to our fatherland." Kurbsky's information establishes the most interesting fact that Russian youths were being sent abroad for learning in the middle of the sixteenth century.[13]

We can limit ourselves to the examples cited to demonstrate that at this time there was some intimacy between the upper layers of the Muscovite populace and the foreign culture of Western Europe. But we can also say that during the reign of Ivan the Terrible the lower levels of the Muscovite populace also became used to contact with "Frenchmen" and "Germans." All the working people who then lived and labored along the routes of commercial exchange between Moscow and foreign countries came into business contact with foreign merchants, served them on their docks and ships and along their land routes and in their *gostinye dvory* - in short, everywhere that overseas trade extended and was maintained. The populace of the towns in which imprisoned foreigners were settled to live and serve became accustomed to seeing them on the streets, in the markets and even in their own homes during times of billeting.

Many of those foreigners who, like unwilling colonists, had been subjected to the control of the Muscovite government, lived in Moscow itself. These, according to Horsey's affirmation, were settled somewhere "on the Bolvanovka near Moscow," probably on the Moskva River, and later were settled in a special settlement on the banks of the river

Yauza, where from 1575-76 they had their own Protestant church. A Pole named Niemojewski, who was a contemporary, says of this settlement that it comprised about one hundred and fifty hovels (huts), of the same type as the black cottages that were customary in Moscow, standing above the river Yauza. Along the river the town mills stood behind fences.

Besides the places that were especially set aside for them, foreigners apparently were able to reside in or move about the various quarters of Moscow itself, as long as they did not become attached to any settlement or household for their work or for other reasons. Interesting features of their daily life are recorded in the diary of the Danish ambassador, Axel Guilderstern, who accompanied Duke Hans to Moscow in 1602. He writes that when the duke first arrived in Moscow, he and his retinue were accommodated in a large inn at the Kremlin. Later the Danes were allotted several more adjoining courts, thus forming one large residence. At first the duke's people were unsuccessful in obtaining permission to move about the town, but later the Danes "had to ask no one's permission and went wherever they wished, strolling about and making purchases." No one prevented them from doing this, although Russians and foreigners living in Moscow were forbidden to speak with the Danes without an official interpreter, and several foreigners were arrested for violating his injunction. But that did not help. "Our people and the local foreigners furtively came together to talk among themselves," says the ambassador. Then the Russians "allowed our nobles and servants to walk and ride on horseback throughout the town as they wished, as long as they took with them a *pristav*. This was observed for two or three days, but afterwards everyone walked or rode wherever he wished without a *pristav*."

As is well known, Duke Hans died in Moscow and was buried near the Protestant church in the foreign settlement on the Yauza. In his detailed description of the funeral, the ambassador recalls that as the solemn funeral procession moved from the Danish court to the settlement, "foreign nobles, military men and merchants, from Moscow as well as from the foreign settlement, joined the procession, some of them in town and some of them out of town, and accompanied the body to the place of burial. Many foreign ladies, girls and female townsfolk also met the funeral train, some of them outside the church and some of them in it."

All these details vividly depict for us the life of the populous and little constrained foreign colony in Moscow at the time of Boris Godunov. We can infer that in Ivan the Terrible's time its life was similar. Only once, in the last years of his life, did Ivan the Terrible "singe" the foreigners living in the German settlement by inflicting upon it a brutal massacre, after which, however, the settlement recovered and lived its life as before. A Catholic outsider who observed this distinctive Protestant community, Jacques Margeret,[14] paints the way of life of this community in interesting strokes. He speaks of the Livonians living in the settlement who, "having lost their fatherland and belongings and become the slaves of a coarse and brutal people subject to the rule of a despotic sovereign, instead of being humbled by the cause of these disasters, bore themselves so proudly, acted so haughtily and dressed so luxuriously that they seemed princes and princesses. When the women attended church they arrayed themselves in nothing but velvet, satin and damask. Every last one of them wore a taffeta dress, even if she had nothing else." The source of the settlement's prosperity, Margeret tells us, was trade, especially trade in wine and illicit traffic in spirits. These petty details demonstrate, it would seem, the extremely favorable material condition of the settlement.

The foreigner in Moscow during the sixteenth century could live in clover, as they say, and was constrained neither by the state nor his surroundings, which he was free to experience and exploit. Only the coarse street throng at times insulted the unfamiliar foreigners with jokes and mockery and adopted nicknames for them, calling their settlement by the unofficial name of "Kokui."[15]

VII   The Ideological Influence of the West

Moscow's contact with the cultured West was not limited to the realm of material and practical borrowings. During the fifteenth and sixteenth centuries, Russia received from the West the ideas from which the mentality of the Renaissance had developed. But in the West this mentality had the brilliance and force of the morning sun, shining brightly upon an awakened intellect. In Russia it flickered for the time being like occasional summer lightning. It did not disperse the darkness of night, but merely frightened the bigoted and superstitious populace. Remote from all cultural centers, crushed by the struggle for the survival of its very national character, enslaved by the Tatar yoke, "Muscovy in the fifteenth century," in the words of Professor M. N. Speransky, "had developed a onesided, backward type of medieval mentality that was based upon a misunderstood or poorly understood Byzantinism: religious and later national exclusiveness; a formal attitude toward the ideas of religion; literalism; ritualism; the absence of education, which was replaced by dogmatism - all the traits of the common medieval cast of mind, now elevated to onesidedness, at times to abnormality." This "orientation, which was imperiously implemented by the church and state in their close union," elicited a counter-orientation, especially where Russian people came into contact with western Europeans on the western boundary of Russia, that is, in Novgorod and Pskov.

We shall say nothing of the early and poorly known heresy of the *strigol'niki*.[16] But the later movement of the "Judaizers" undoubtedly contained elements of western European rationalism. It was broadly espoused by the circle of Novgorodian writers; it spread to Moscow and penetrated even the ruling class of the state. Special efforts had to be made by the church hierarchy and secular authorities to cope with the "heresy" and to suppress it. The heresy was condemned. Its adherents suffered, but they created an attitude of criticism and scepticism in regard to religious dogma and the ecclesiastical order that did not die.[17] This was inherited by other circles that were less radical and did not embrace heresy and apostasy, but were inclined to believe only in what "was in accord with my reason, was well pleasing to God and of benefit to my soul."

In these circles reflection led to the desire to know not only one's own written language, but also the western languages that were relevant to literary activity. For this reason interest in translations arose, and these could be undertaken even unofficially. At the end of the fifteenth century several works of theology were translated, as well as learned tracts (the "Logic" and "Cosmography") and astrological works. "The renewal of the intellectual life of Muscovite Russia began in this manner," says M. N. Speransky. "By the middle of the sixteenth century the results of this work were already beginning to show clearly." The struggle of two orientations, one progressive, the other conservative, became evident. Supporters of each felt that "the old had passed away," but differed in their understanding of what should replace it. Some reached out to the West, "gradually increasing the fund of western literature in Russian use and thereby preparing the final triumph of western culture in Russia." Others labored to "check the influx of freethinkers, to demonstrate their uselessness and show that the old principles were not obsolete, but that they were vital and had merely been forgotten through carelessness." Ivan the Terrible and his spiritual mentor, Metropolitan Macarius, belonged to the orientation that determined not to borrow from abroad but to rejuvenate ancient principles.[18]

But the power of the new cultural currents is seen in Ivan the Terrible himself. Although he defended ancient beliefs and ideals, he himself was so drawn to the side of the "barbarian" novelties that he aroused, as we have seen, the astonishment and indignation of Muscovite nationalists, who considered that "every barbarian in our state had him in his grasp." The infantile state of cultural and political thought could not accommodate these diverse views of life. Innovations in the world of ideas and belief were feared, even as the material aspects of life abroad were being borrowed willingly.

VIII Foreigners in Moscow at the Time of Boris Godunov

Ivan the Terrible died at the beginning of 1584. His death ended the terror that had shaken the Muscovite state, and the ruling power passed into the gentle and deft hands of Boris Godunov. Though a pupil of Ivan the Terrible, Godunov did not inherit Ivan's inclination to tyranny and terror. But he did adopt much of Ivan's political system and his interest in and love for the products of western culture. All foreigners with one voice speak of Boris' great kindness toward them. He received with extraordinary kindness foreigners who, out of need or good will, came to serve Russia in business or trade. He conversed at length with his foreign physicians and with diplomats from European governments. He was noted for his religious tolerance of all Protestant doctrines. Moreover, he appreciated the value of learning and learned men. As in the time of Ivan the Terrible, measures were taken in Boris' day to attract learned men and technicians to Russia. It was commonly said abroad that Boris desired to build a university in Moscow. Finally, Boris urgently longed to become related to one of the European dynasties and twice attempted to arrange a match between his daughter, Ksenia, and Swedish and Dutch princes.

Unfortunately, this attempt at matchmaking was unsuccessful. The Swedish prince, Gustav, who had been banished from Sweden and was invited to Moscow "for an appanage," proved to be an awkward and unseemly person. For Ksenia's sake he had no inclination to change either his faith or his morganatic involvement, which he transferred to Moscow from Danzig. He therefore had to be removed to Uglich, where he would be out of the Tsar's sight. A Danish prince, Duke Hans of Holstein, was much more satisfactory. But upon his arrival in Moscow he fell ill for a month and a half, then died. The Danish ambassador, Axel Guilderstern, who was attached to the duke, testifies to Boris' unusual kindness to the embassy and his deep grief at the loss of the duke. At the grave Boris lamented in tears: "Alas, Duke Hans, my light and my consolation! Because of our sins we were unable to keep him!" Supposedly, the Tsar could hardly speak from crying.

During Boris' time the Muscovite government first had recourse to an enlightened measure that later became customary. It sent abroad to "learn various languages and reading and writing" several Russian boys, young noblemen. They were to learn "strictly how to read and write the language" of the country to which they were sent. We know from records that five were sent to Lübeck and four to England. According to private accounts, eighteen were sent in all, six each to England, France and Germany. Interestingly, none of those sent returned with the desired results of study. Several died. Others proved to be "refractory and did not listen to the lessons," and even "ran away" from the teachers "for some unknown reason." Some of them accepted the "lessons" but remained abroad forever. One of these, Nikifor Alferievich Grigoriev, became a priest in England, "a noble member of the Episcopalian clergy," and lived to old age. In 1643 during the Puritan movement he even suffered for his steadfastness in his new belief and lost his parish in Huntingdonshire.

Russian diplomats abroad tried in vain to raise the question of bringing these apostates home. But neither the boys themselves nor the authorities of their new fatherlands agreed to their return to Russia.[19]

For their part, however, the Muscovite authorities of Boris' day readily extended hospitality not only to foreigners who came to Moscow strictly because of practical concerns, but also to those who came, for example, to learn the language. Those who were motivated by simple curiosity and came "to learn and look at the customs of the state" were also welcome. We know that in 1600 "the French foreigner, Jean Parcet, who was eighteen years of age, and the Englishman William Collier, both young boys," were studying the Russian language in Moscow. At the same time the Russian ambassador to London, Grigory Ivanovich Mikulin, cordially invited some travelers to Moscow — three brothers who were "princes of the Moravian lands and who in their homeland were called barons." He explained to them that Tsar Boris readily accepted foreigners for service and that they "live in his realm with great salary, in peace and serenity, and enjoy a prosperous life." Mikulin asked these "prince barons" how they wished to go to Tsar Boris in Moscow, "whether to serve in his name or merely to visit His Imperial Majesty in his land." Obviously, Boris fully allowed enlightened foreigners, "who traveled throughout various states for learning and to look at the customs of the state at their leisure," the opportunity of visiting Moscow out of pure curiosity.

Boris' commercial policy in regard to foreigners was distinguished by great tenacity and skill. He knew how to promote firmly the interests of the state, even while he flattered foreign merchants by showing them every mark of kindness. Englishmen were very well satisfied with him, for after Ivan the Terrible's death he treated them better than he did other dignitaries and rendered them much patronage and service. But neither during his early regency nor during his reign did the English trading company recover the exclusive privileges that Ivan the Terrible had accorded it in 1569, prior to his disagreements with Queen Elizabeth. Boris firmly held to the view that Russian harbors should be open to all countries and that the right to come to the mouth of the Northern Dvina should be equally enjoyed by traders of all states. When the English trading company attempted to renew its solicitation for the exclusive use of the Dvina route, it was pointed out that the Muscovite government considered it unwise to bar the many people from many states who came to Archangel simply to accommodate the English merchants, and that the English ought to be satisfied with the exclusive privilege they alone enjoyed of exemption from duty in Russian markets. Thus the English company remained, as it were, most favored; but this did not prevent Boris from showing kindness to all other foreigners.

This tendency had been evident among the ruling circles of Moscow even before Boris became head of the government. In July, 1584 an English merchant who did not belong to the privileged company wrote to another that "trade is free" in the Muscovite state since Ivan the Terrible's death. From all parts merchants are being invited to come with their goods "to trade, each for himself, according to his own will" (this is how Russian translators rendered the English speech). "Have no fear. Everything will be good for us in Muscovy." Boris fully justified these expectations of the foreigners. During his reign everything really "was good in Muscovy," and foreigners never tired of praising his attitudes and disposition toward them. The foreign colony in Moscow under Boris experienced great prosperity, as is attested by the memoirs of foreigners who felt at home in Moscow, such as Isaac Massa (a Dutchman) and Conrad Bussow.

IX Foreigners in Moscow at the Time of the First Pretender. The Massacre of Poles in May, 1606

We have seen that to this point Europe was represented in Russia by those who conducted trade, by military and civilian prisoners and by all sorts of technicians needed by the Muscovite authorities. Visitors such as the above mentioned "princes of the Moravian lands," who came "at their leisure," because of their curiosity to see other states, were as yet unknown in Moscow. These visitors appeared - and then in a merry and noisy band - only at the time of Tsar Dimitry Ivanovich, who had himself "assumed the name of Tsar" and who is therefore called the Pretender.

The Pretender was undoubtedly Russian, and not a Livonian or Pole. But his claim to the throne of Russia began and developed in Poland with the support of the Polish government and some segments of Polish society. Under conditions of "complete freedom" he first recruited for himself in Poland a small Polish-Lithuanian military force, then established working relations with the Muscovite Ukraine, where he supported a movement against Godunov's Muscovite government that could be useful to himself. In August, 1604 he opened a campaign against Boris. Rebellious Cossack bands moved north from the Muscovite Ukraine. To link up with these the Pretender and his Polish detachment set out from Poland by way of Kiev and Chernigov. The junction was expected somewhere in the region of Orel or Tula. But it did not occur, because Godunov's troops smashed those of the Pretender and drove them to Putivl. Almost all the Polish troops were scattered. The Pretender retained only a few hundred volunteers out of three or four thousand.

It was in Putivl that the Pretender received word of Boris' death and the overthrow of his son, Feodor. When the Pretender was recognized as Tsar Dimitry by Moscow and entered the capital in triumph and sat upon "the throne of his forefathers," all the Polish troops that were serving him were settled in Moscow in one "ambassadorial court," that is, in the residence area where foreign embassies to Moscow were usually lodged.

When he entered the Kremlin palace the Pretender brought with him many foreigners, with whom he neither wished nor was able to sever the relations begun in Poland. Around him, along with boiars and Muscovite aristocrats, were Polish retainers, including his secretary, Buczynski, and the latter's brother, both of whom he relied upon to conduct relations with Poland. The military chaplains Czyrzowski and

Lawicki, who had been attached to Dimitry's Polish troops, remained in Moscow after the demobilization of the Polish troops. These two Jesuits were commissioned by their religious superiors to ensure that the Pretender did not leave the Catholic Church, into whose bosom he had been received during the spring of 1604.

The demobilization of the Polish bands that had accompanied the Pretender to Moscow did not force all Poles to depart from Moscow for their homeland. Part of them remained in Moscow and continued to serve the Tsar in the capacity of a guards detachment. All these people were settled throughout Moscow and felt themselves lords of the situation. They considered that the Pretender owed something to his Polish noble "comrades" for their labors and assistance. And it seems that the Pretender shared their opinion and indulged the Poles. He allowed them their excesses and left unpunished the offences they inflicted upon the populace. He even rubbed shoulders with them in their soldiers' pranks and carousing. For the first time foreigners in Moscow seemed not dependents, but the most important citizens. They looked down on Russians and considered the road to Moscow open to any foreigner. In his outward appearance, his dress and manners, the Tsar of Moscow himself appeared a foreigner to the Muscovite crowd. He destroyed, as it were, the centuries-old obstacle between Russia and the West in customs and faith. His predecessors, the sovereigns of the sixteenth century, had been close only with people of the Protestant persuasion, but the Pretender opened the road to Moscow to Catholics as well, who, in the mind of the contemporary Russian, were "soul destroying wolves."

In general, religious differences were unimportant to the Pretender. He favored Catholic Poles and Protestant Germans alike. His court guard, which was composed of foreigners, included people of various religions and countries. In addition to Poles it contained French and Germans. One foreigner, Bussow, has left us an interesting description of this combined detachment. It comprised three teams of one hundred men, each distinguished by its arms and clothing. The first hundred, the gunners, went about in velvet and gold, were richly supplied and were esteemed the elite. Its captain was the Frenchman, Margeret, a typical adventurer of the time, who had served Henry IV in France, the

Emperor in Germany, the King in Poland and the Tsars Boris and Dimitry in Moscow. A master not only of the sword and musket but of the pen as well, he has left us a fascinating and intelligent book with a description of events and institutions in Moscow *(Etat de l'Empire de Russie et Grande Duchè de Moscovie,* Paris, 1607).

The other two hundred bodyguards were under the command of the German, Knutsen, and the Scot, Vandeman. These were armed with halberds, dressed smartly and gaudily, were supplied to their full satisfaction and, according to one contemporary, showed no little pride and had upturned noses.[20] To have this armed force always close at hand, the Pretender lodged them in houses near the Kremlin, evicting for this purpose priests from the Arbatsky and Prechistensky sections of the city.

One has to fix firmly in mind the situation the Pretender created, in order to understand the sudden change in Muscovite life. The populace of Moscow no longer felt themselves masters of their own city. Not only in the "courts" (town estates), which had customarily been set aside for the billeting of embassies and arriving foreigners, but in private homes, in churches, in the Kremlin itself and in and around the court - everywhere Muscovites saw Poles, "Lithuanians" and "Germans" in the capacity of permanent inhabitants, serving Tsar Dimitry or being maintained at his expense. Nor were they ashamed to show Moscow that they dominated the city and that "they enjoyed the favor of the sovereign."

According to many recollections by contemporaries, the foreigners of the Pretender's day did not restrain themselves at all. One of the Poles who was in Moscow at the time, Stadnicki, says honestly that "the Muscovites were greatly disturbed by the debauchery of the Poles, who began to treat them like their subjects, attacked them, quarreled with them, insulted them, beat them while drunk and insulted women and girls." The raucous carousing of the foreigners, during which toasts were accompanied by shooting, frightened the Russian populace. Muscovite merchants reached a general agreement not to sell foreigners "poison" (gunpowder) when they looked for it in the commercial stalls. Against this background there developed in Moscow the mood that was responsible for the brutal massacre of foreigners, chiefly Poles and Lithuanians, that occurred in May, 1606.

The marriage of the Pretender and Marina occasioned a new influx of foreign strangers into Moscow. The bride was accompanied to the royal "merriment" not only by her relatives but also by guests, invited and uninvited, and all sorts of traders - from prominent jewellers to petty confectioners. Some came seeking honor and diversion; others, profitable business; still others, simply a piece of the bread that was lacking in their homeland. There are still extant several very interesting stories concerning the weeks of this wedding, which agitated Moscow to its breaking point. During these days, Muscovites beheld many things of interest and things hitherto unknown to them, which entertained and amazed them. But with all this they also experienced influences that in the end roused them against the newly-arrived guests, and against their own Tsar as well.

Pan Yury Mniszech and his daughter, Marina, traveled to Moscow with a complete army. Their train numbered 1,969 men and 1,960 horses, although we must note that these figures are minimal and that the more reliable total is more than 2,000 men with a corresponding number of horses. When they were near Moscow Pan Yury overtook Marina and reached the city several days earlier. A magnificent reception was arranged in his honor. Troops were drawn up in lines and formed a great escort ("of about a thousand and a half Muscovites"), in which the Tsar himself rode incognito. The voevoda Mniszech was brought to the Kremlin on a floating bridge that had been especially constructed on boats across the Moskva River. The next day he was presented to the Tsar at a festive audience and greeted the Tsar with a florid speech, which caused the Pretender, in the words of Martin Stadnicki, who was an eyewitness, "to cry like a beaver, wiping his eyes with his kerchief." But a Muscovite diplomat, the *dumnyi diak* Afanasy Vlasiev, remarked that "the Pan voevoda talks too much."

But this triumph was merely the prelude to what was to follow. Marina's entry into Moscow was much more magnificent. The entire official class of Moscow, the entire garrison of the city and the entire Polish retinue of Pan Mniszech moved out to meet her. Marina awaited the beginning of the ceremony in a field, in the "snowlike" tents that Boris Godunov had built outside the town for all sorts of festivities.

They seemed to comprise an entire little town of highly adorned canvas. It was said that on the eve of Marina's arrival the Pretender galloped to these tents incognito to greet the noblewoman.

On the day of her arrival (May 2, 1606), the Polish embassy that had been sent to the royal wedding by King Sigismund overtook Marina at these tents. And it opened the procession, provocatively for Muscovites, as the ambassadors rode "in the military manner, with their horses covered with trappings and pikes in their hands, not according to ambassadorial custom, but in military fashion." Behind the embassy Marina advanced to Moscow. At the city limits she was met by a gala carriage that was richly adorned and was so tall that she entered it by a ladder of five steps. This "vessel" was drawn by twelve dapple-gray horses, one of which was that color naturally, while the rest had been tinted.[21] Throughout the procession were many horses that had been tinged unusual colors. Behind Marina's carriage advanced additional lavish carriages carrying her suite of women. Before it, and in the forefront of the procession, rode Polish detachments, the "friends" of the Mniszechs, and behind them were the Muscovite boiars and nobles, comprising a well-dressed crowd of several thousand. Bringing up the rear were cavalry units of Marina's Polish escort, riding in armor and fully armed, with trumpets and flutes, again "like warriors," in the manner of the Polish embassy that had passed an hour earlier. The garrison of Moscow was stretched along the entire route of the procession and crowds of people stood, staggered by the unprecedented spectacle of this triumphant, we might even say victorious, entry of these armed foreigners into Moscow.

Before the Kremlin the procession was greeted by music that was native in character: trumpets, kettledrums and drums "as great as wine casks," which "were banged with one hand." The zeal that the musicians had for their playing produced the impression of the noise of a water mill. "The noise and din lasted a long time, until it became unbearable." The procession entered the Kremlin and stopped near the Monastery of the Assumption, where Marina was lodged until her marriage to the Tsar. The rest of the Poles were accommodated throughout the entire city, in all its quarters, far apart from each other. We might say that they captured all Moscow.

The final days before the wedding (which took place on May 8) were spent in official receptions and private banquets in the palace, during which the Pretender's intimate closeness to his newly arrived guests was strikingly evident. All Moscow was disturbed by the noisy movements of the guests and their unseemly conduct. Polish dominance was expressed even in petty matters of palace etiquette. During all these days, for example, the palace kitchen, along with the keys to its larders and cellars, was surrendered to Polish cooks, because Marina did not like Russian food. The Muscovite populace saw only these external manifestations of foreign overlordship. But people who were closer to the government were able to observe other indications of the menace that faced them.

During the days that preceded the wedding the Pretender tried to resolve the virtually insoluble problem of the marriage of an Orthodox Tsar to an "unbaptized" Catholic woman.[22] Marina did not wish to adopt the Russian faith. On the contrary, she had been inspired while in Poland with the hope that in time she could bring the Tsar and all of Russia into the bosom of Catholicism. The Pretender was therefore faced with the prospect of arranging his marriage without the ceremony that would unite his bride to Orthodoxy. He escaped from this difficulty by arranging a special ceremony of betrothal in the banquet hall of the palace, prior to the church ceremony. Afterwards there took place in the Cathedral of the Assumption a rite hitherto unseen in Russia, the coronation of a Tsarina with anointing, an action that was meant to replace the ritual that would have joined Marina to Orthodoxy. Mass followed the coronation, and after Mass the wedding rites. But those experienced in canon law were chagrined to note that the young couple abstained from the Eucharist. From this it was learned that Marina had not been united to the Orthodox Church.

To the populace the affair remained obscure and confused by the complexity of the ecclesiastical ceremonies. Muscovite eyewitnesses merely noticed that the Tsar went from the palace to the cathedral surrounded by Poles and that many Polish guests were admitted to the church, while common Russian folk were admitted neither to the Cathedral of the Assumption nor to the Kremlin, which was flooded with foreign visitors. The true significance of the matter, however, was explained to the crowds by agitators who, with Prince Vasily Ivanovich Shuisky and other boiars, were preparing to overthrow the Pretender. They made good use of the days of nuptial "merriment" and quickly brought the mood of Muscovites to a revolutionary boil.

Their task presented no special difficulties. Neither the Pretender nor his guests understood the general setting in which their "merriment" proceeded. Only serious Poles from the official Polish embassy sent to Moscow by the king correctly evaluated Moscow's mood. They kept their "Polish court" in a state of siege and sent cautious warnings to the palace. The rest of the Polish brethren danced frivolously on a volcano. From the mouths of the Poles themselves we have indications of how they behaved noisily, dissolutely and tactlessly and constrained official Muscovite personages in various ways. Concerning their contemptuous attitude toward the Russian faith and church we have Pan Stadnicki's personal testimony concerning a sermon he himself is supposed to have heard in the village of Viazemy in the environs of Moscow. He recounts that the priest glorified St. Nicholas the Wonderworker and that "he concluded his address by saying that, if God were to grow old, Nicholas would become God." To this a deacon retorted, "what the priest babbles is nonsense, for God can neither die nor grow old." To which the priest replied, "what the deacon says is foolish, for if God cannot grow old, then Nicholas will not become God, as I said."[23] This story Stadnicki set in rhyme and cited as a factual event to which he had been an eyewitness. It illustrates, of course, his extremely frivolous and cynical attitude toward the religion of our country.

Because of their own experiences Muscovites attributed similar attitudes to other Polish panies as well. At the Pretender's coronation the Polish ambassador who accompanied him as he entered the church doffed his plumed hat. Whereupon the *dumnyi diak,* Afanasy Vlasiev, went to him and suggested that he hold the ambassador's hat. But when Vlasiev was given the hat, it was taken from the church, lest the Pole wear it there. From this incident grew a whole story. The Poles themselves claimed that the affair of the hat's removal "had been planned in advance, before they entered the church," for the Russians had feared that "the ambassador would put the hat back on his head out of disrespect for the place where the ceremonies were held and the person of the grand prince."

But this fear was apparently well founded. Russian boiars later brought accusations against the Polish guests in Moscow to the Polish diplomats, charging that they had grossly violated the ceremonial rituals of the church and had scandalized the religious sensitivities of native inhabitants.[24]

The movement to rouse the masses against the Tsar who had not baptized his wife, against Marina, who had not wished to exchange her "Roman faith" for the "true faith," against the "Lithuanians" and Poles, who had become masters of the palace, quickly made extraordinary progress. In the days following the royal wedding, while feast followed feast in the palace and the Pretender, in Hussar's dress, amused himself with his Polish guests, Moscow was already seething. On the night of May 14 there was such disorder on the streets that Polish soldiers "were on the ready and armed, as for battle." On the next day, May 15, a street disturbance erupted because of some minor outrage committed by a Pole. By May 16 the Poles all knew with certainty that "the Russians had begun a serious revolt." Only the Pretender refused to believe that his situation was precarious. He smiled at all warnings and presumptuously ridiculed the "Caesar" Rudolph, the Pope himself and even his benefactor, the Polish king. He graciously remarked of the latter, by the way, that he was not as great an idiot as Emperor Rudolph. But fate laughed at him. At dawn on May 17 Moscow finally rose and the coup was completed.

As far as we can conclude from the reports of eyewitnesses, the plan of the boiars who had plotted against the Tsar was to launch the populace against the Poles, then direct it against the foreigners who were scattered throughout the various sections of the city, thereby depriving the Pretender of Polish assistance. Then the palace would be rushed and the Tsar and his retainers would be dealt with. This plan succeeded completely. The crowd began to attack the Polish guests throughout the city, while a detachment of boiars burst into the Kremlin and seized the palace, where the Tsar was killed and Marina and her retinue were arrested.

Polish memoirs recount interesting details of the massacre. The courts where foreigners lived suffered pillage and violence. Those who did not resist were most often simply killed or beaten and covered with wounds by pillagers. Wherever there was resistance a siege and a real battle began. Only those Poles survived who were able to defend themselves until matters at the Kremlin reached a climax. After the boiars dealt with the Pretender and seized the Kremlin and the palace, they rushed to end the massacre in the city and put an end everywhere to the bloodshed and pillaging. The Polish embassy and notable Poles and their servants, who had remained safe from the crowds in their own courts, were placed under guard by the boiars and then, like prisoners of war, were distributed throughout various towns. Polish calculations claim that during the massacre more than 500 men were killed, while a private Muscovite report claimed about 3,500.[25] It would seem that the Polish figure is much closer to the truth, for the Poles tell us exactly the number of victims in the suites of many pani, according to their own careful count.

Not only notable Poles died and suffered in the massacre. The Russians beat all foreigners at hand, not only armed men but even the peaceful merchants who had been invited to Moscow by the Pretender's secretary, Buczynski, as well as Polish magnates. Thus there perished at this time the jeweller from Milan, Cellari, several German merchants from Augsburg along with their servants, and two wine merchants from the town of Krosno in Galicia, who had brought Hungarian wine to Moscow. The merchant Baptist, from Cracow, was covered with wounds and left for dead. All the wares of these people were either ransacked or confiscated. The merchants who survived the massacre were, along with other foreigners, scattered throughout various towns. In this manner, Moscow was purged of the objectionable guests summoned by the Pretender. The old inhabitants of Moscow, the foreigners of the German settlement, were spared the massacre and remained its detached witnesses.

X Foreign Intervention During the Years of the Time of Troubles

The attempt to subordinate Moscow to Catholicism and Polish culture was overturned by one violent surge of a popular wave. The calculations of the King of Poland and the hopes of the Papal Curia to place a Catholic Tsar on the throne of Moscow and to bring the Muscovite state into the political sphere of influence of Rome and Poland collapsed. Moscow remained true to its ancient hatred of the Papacy and its implacable hostility toward Poles and Lithuanians.

After the massacre of May, 1606, Moscow treated all the pani who had survived as her prisoners. In Moscow itself, as in Rostov, Yaroslavl, Kostroma, Vologda and Beloozero, they languished under difficult conditions, waiting for the diplomatic intervention of the Polish Commonwealth to free them from their incarceration and return them to their homeland. But even while oppression was being visited upon the Poles by their rude jailors, these unwilling Polish colonies in the land of Muscovy were able to play something of a cultural role. The Polish nobles, as well as their servants, were still able to move about the town in which they had been settled, to go out on the streets and into the markets, to talk with the people and even to try to persuade *streltsy* and peasants to carry news from one group of prisoners to others. Thus one of the *streltsy* in Moscow was bribed by Pan Peter Stadnicki to carry secretly from Moscow to Pan Martin Stadnicki in Beloozero "the Italian Petrarch," disguised as a prayerbook, in the leather binding of which was pasted a most interesting description of the siege of Moscow by Bolotnikov at the end of 1606. This sort of interchange between the townspeople and the foreigners taught the Russians to appreciate the prisoners' point of view, destroyed the fear they had of them, made personal influences possible and prepared for what was to follow in the next few years - the massive incursion of the Poles at Tushino into Great Russia.

As we know, the Time of Troubles did not come to an end with the May massacre and the accession of Shuisky, but, on the contrary, entered a new and more complicated and difficult phase. The populace of the southern districts of Muscovy (the Ukrainians), who had been stirred up by the first Pretender, did not believe that he had really perished and, in the name of the surviving "Tsar Dimitry," moved on Moscow against the boiar Tsar, Vasily [Shuisky]. The first push by the rebels failed. Tsar Vasily repelled their attack and after a difficult campaign of almost a year, forced the rebel "brigands" (for this is how people who violated the law were termed at the time) into complete capitulation after their leaders, with Bolotnikov[26] at their head, had perished in 1607.

But there immediately followed a new uprising under the leadership of a second Pretender, who was joined not only by Muscovite "brigands" but by Poles and Lithuanians as well. These Poles (Prince Roman Rozynski, Pan Jan Peter Sapieha and others) assumed complete control over the enterprise, became its military leaders, led the insurgents to Moscow itself, which they invested, and in 1608 settled down near the capital in two bases, in the villages of Tushino and Dmitrov. From here they mounted the conquest of Great Russia. Lithuanian and Polish detachments spread throughout the entire central Povolzhie, from Tver almost to Nizhnii Novgorod, crossed the Volga, reached Vologda and not only captured the town but even settled in its rural districts. They devoted themselves thereafter to simple plunder or to requisitioning for their troops.

To oppose them Shuisky assembled not only Russian troops from the parts of the state that were most loyal to him but even hired foreign detachments of mercenaries, who had been supplied with armor and firearms by the Swedish government in return for certain territorial concessions. With this "armored company" the Muscovite commander, Prince Mikhail V. Skopin-Shuisky, launched a campaign from Novgorod to Tver and Kaliazin, from there to Aleksandrova Sloboda, and then, in 1609, to Moscow. The purpose of this campaign was to unite with other troops loyal to Shuisky and to move with them against the second Pretender. During this campaign Skopin taught his troops the methods of regular warfare under the direction of foreign instructors. Thus both sides in the Russian civil war operated under the influence and direction of foreigners. Never had Great Russia found so many of them in her bosom. According to contemporary evidence, the Pretender had as many as 20,000 Polish and Lithuanian troops, while the Swedish mercenaries with Skopin numbered 10,000 to 15,000. And this entire mass of people was spread throughout the broad expanse of the Muscovite state, with the exception of its remote northern and eastern borderlands. Relying upon their military superiority, they behaved as conquerers always behave in a conquered land.

The subsequent course of the Russian Time of Troubles led to formal intervention in Russian affairs by neighboring powers. This intervention culminated with the King of Poland conquering the western and southwestern regions of the Muscovite state (from Velikie Luki to Viaz'ma, Briansk and Chernigov), while the Swedes occupied the entire region of Novgorod. Seeing no other way out of their civil war, the Muscovites recognized a Polish prince as their Tsar. But he did not come to the city; rather, a Polish garrison occupied Moscow in 1610. The people of Novgorod also summoned to "the state of Novgorod" a Swedish prince, recommending him also to the Muscovites. It appeared that the unified Russian state had ceased to exist.

A contemporary remarked that no book has ever recounted "such punishments being visited on any monarch, nor on tsardoms or principalities, as those that have fallen upon most exalted Russia." There was no longer a state, but merely its "relics." There was no longer a people, but only "the relics of a Christian family." "Alien hands" had seized everything. The King of Poland, Sigismund, considered himself the sovereign of Moscow, which he had captured with the rest of its realm. His agents directed affairs in Moscow, using military force. The King of Sweden, Charles, looked upon Novgorod as his own province and hoped for the dynastic union of Sweden and Russia. Only the Pomorie and the Lower Reaches[27] of Muscovy did not experience foreign rule firsthand, simply because the Swedes and the Poles did not reach the northern and eastern borderlands of Russia. All the rest of the land saw the "alien hands" with its own eyes and obeyed them against its will.

But the Russian North was also desired by foreigners who knew it. During the civil war commerce died out at Archangel. Foreign merchants who were caught up in the Time of Troubles either hurriedly made for their homelands or, in Moscow, Vologda and Archangel, inactively awaited the outcome of events. Some of them sat out the

Time of Troubles by remaining in Moscow throughout its entire siege. In Vologda foreign merchants joined the local defense council in 1609, in order to work against Tushino "with other chiefs and military men who were of the same mind." John Merrick, the experienced observer who had known Moscow since the days of Ivan the Terrible and Godunov, and kept the English well informed of events there, was still in Kholmogory in 1611. Dutch merchants, no less than the English, followed the course of events in Moscow. One of them, Isaac Massa, published an extraordinary account of the Russian Time of Troubles. He left the center of the Muscovite state only in 1609, when the road from Yaroslavl to the White Sea had been cleared of Tushinites and all foreigners rushed to the sea at Archangel, where "they found their English and Dutch ships, which they had expected never to see again."

The impact of news from Moscow elicited from the English a definite plan to make an English protectorate of the Russian North and the Volga route to the Caspian, that is, the very parts of the Muscovite state that were not occupied by Poles and Swedes and were not under the control of the Cossacks. The author of this plan, which probably originated in 1612, seems to have been the above mentioned John Merrick. He was banished because the Russians themselves consulted him about this very question, and he dared say that the seizure of important northern Russian towns might be carried out by English forces even without the consent of the Russians. There is information that the King of England, James I, "was captivated by the plan to send an army to Russia, that he might administer it through a deputy." In connection with this matter, at the beginning of 1613 he did send John Merrick and William Russell to Moscow as his deputies. But they did not even have the opportunity to begin their speeches about a protectorate, because they found in Moscow Tsar Michael Feodorovich, who had already been chosen "by all the land."

Along with these governmental plans private proposals to meddle in Russian affairs matured in the West. During his march from Yaroslavl to Moscow Prince Dimitry Pozharsky[28] and his comrades had to contend with one of these attempts. Before him appeared "a foreigner from the Scottish land, James Shaw," who was a messenger sent by a large company of adventurers of various nationalities commanded by "a head voevoda and boiar, Adrian Floderan, a Lithuanian from Caesar's land." He also had several colonels - Germans, French and English. Among them was Margeret, who had served the first Pretender and is already known to us. Shaw announced that this entire company was making its way into Russia through Archangel "to secure a treaty for the hiring of foreign troops," in the hope that the company "could then enter the entire land, to their great joy." But Pozharsky's government thought otherwise and declined to hire "the commander Adrian and his comrades," declaring that they "would themselves defend the Russian state from the Polish people without hired men." The Russian people had more than once experienced the unreliability of hired troops and did not trust such "turncoats" as Margeret, for they knew that in earlier times he "had robbed and caused more evil than the Polish people" and had fled from Moscow "after having stolen many riches."

The idea that they had to pass through the Time of Troubles with their own forces and without intervention and assistance from outsiders, it seems, strongly preoccupied Russian minds until Moscow was liberated from the Polish garrison. During the difficult time of "devastation," that is, at the time when their society had completely disintegrated in 1610-11, Russians were willing to recognize any rule, if only it could end the Time of Troubles. Some supported the Polish prince; others began negotiations to invite a Swedish prince; others discussed with English agents the idea of the English protectorate; still others considered the possibility of inviting the Hapsburg, Maximilian. But when Moscow "was cleansed by God, through the Russian people," and it became possible to summon a *zemskii sobor* to elect a Tsar, this *sobor* first of all resolved not to seek a Tsar from abroad, but to choose him from "the great clans" of Moscow.

From the Time of Troubles Russian society derived close familiarity with foreigners. But this familiarity did not result in inner rapprochement. Foreigners were not always considered enemies, but they never seemed to be true friends.

Chapter Two

THE FIRST HALF OF THE SEVENTEENTH CENTURY

I The Early Years of the New Dynasty and the Question of Borrowing

The Russian people emerged from the Time of Troubles materially devastated and spiritually shaken. The new Tsar, Michael Feodorovich, faced many extremely difficult problems, especially that of restoring balance among the social classes, which had not yet cooled from the passions of the struggle, and repairing the economic life of the country and consolidating the administrative organs to the point that they could work toward the establishment of internal order and the defense of the state. These practical problems were intertwined with problems of another order. Because of the Time of Troubles the Russian people were "reduced in spirit and shattered" in their customs and conceptions. The collapse of ancient social principles, the incursion of masses of foreigners into Russian life, the civil war and all the "treasons" connected with it - all this shattered the old outlook, shook the former confidence that Russia was a nation chosen by God, "a new Israel," and opened the way for foreign influences on Russian minds. It seemed essential to return the minds of the people to the old ways of ancient piety and national exclusiveness. In all its enactments the new Muscovite government tried to retreat to the old order - "as it had been in the days of former great sovereigns." It did not yet sense that the Time of Troubles had overturned forever that old order and that the life of the future had to be fashioned anew upon a combination of old principles and new elements.

One of these elements was the foreigners, the representatives of the

European community, with their technology, capital and culture. During the years of the Time of Troubles they had spread throughout the Muscovite state to such an extent that they had become familiar to every Russian. Despite the feelings that they aroused in Orthodox people, the Orthodox were nevertheless forced to admit that without the foreigners they could not progress. Their many military encounters with hostile detachments especially convinced the Russians that their military proficiency was much inferior to that of the foreigners, who had developed arms into a particularly highly cultivated profession. Under Vasily Shuisky, Russians had first used European troops who had been hired by simple contracts and gradually came to recognize that without such troops they could not prosecute the war, just as they recognized that they had to imitate the military technology of foreigners. And this technology became the most important object of borrowing in the first years after the Time of Troubles.

But other foreign products also attracted the attention of the Russian people, who had become practiced during the Time of Troubles in seeing with their own eyes the customs of foreigners. As Russia recovered from the shocks it had suffered, it put forward a demand for the most diverse articles of foreign production, from musical instruments and clocks to metal items of fine workmanship and pharmaceutical drugs unknown in Russia. Moscow's demands pleased the English and Dutch merchants and "experts" of all nationalities, who appeared in great numbers at the Northern Dvina after internal peace returned to the Muscovite state. Thanks to them, foreign commercial capital entered Russian life on a much greater scale and with much greater influence than before the Time of Troubles. Because of general impoverishment in Russia, foreign capital became the main strength of the Russian economy, and the Muscovite government inevitably had to rely heavily upon it in its efforts to overcome the economic crisis. Foreign merchants became the decisive factors in Russian trade and the suppliers of silver (and even of Russian coins) for Russian markets. They acquired such dominance over Russian business life that the native commercial class persistently began to seek protection from the government, until it did achieve several legislations that limited the trade privileges of foreigners.

In this manner the foreign professional soldier, the "master technician" and the merchant were treated as a necessary part of Russian life. A great many foreigners settled in Moscow and other Russian commercial cities and, closely linked with Russians in matters of business and everyday affairs, could not help but influence their neighbors.

In two respects the foreign influence proved irresistible. First, the foreigners were much more knowledgeable and talented than the Russians. Willingly or unwillingly, Russians had to learn from them, not teach them. Secondly, the foreigners lived more freely and more gaily. Under the ascetic influence of ancient Byzantinism, the Russian clergy persecuted every manifestation of healthy joy in living. It considered sinful everything that departed from the outlook of the church. It threatened with eternal torment innocent merriment in which it could detect anything heretical or "Mahometan." Only during the brief periods of great holidays did the Russian people unwind in drunken sprees, when they startled foreign observers by their spontaneous licentiousness in wild merriment and revelry. But Russia regarded this as a "fall," or sin, which one had to confess or for which one had to suffer in hell. But foreigners lived in their own milieu, without the fear of hell or the depressing notion that impending and implacable retribution followed any free manifestation of a buoyant spirit. And these characteristics of an epicurean community, hitherto unseen by the Russian people, inevitably attracted them, much as a ray of sunlight attracts one in the darkness of a cave.

Once they had fallen under the charm of western culture, Russians were necessarily brought into contact with its foundation, the Protestant mentality, which freed the soul from inner slavery and appeared in Russia in the guise not only of moderate Lutheranism but also of more radical and rationalistic sects. The Orthodox began to fear these heretical deviations and to oppose them. Yet even in this devout work they were unable to manage with their own resources, but had to seek the help of Orthodox Ukrainians from the Polish Commonwealth. The Ukrainians, however, appeared in Moscow not merely as learned representatives of Orthodoxy but as bearers of a Polish culture that was just as alien to Russia. They became the conductors of a cultural influence that was especially foreign.

If to these we add the people who came from the Orthodox East to beg alms and serve or live in Moscow (and who brought with them their own cultural style), we have a complete enumeration of the cultural influences that developed in Moscow by the middle of the seventeenth century, after the Time of Troubles. The realm of the military, the world of commerce, the rudiments of industrial techniques, the problems of faith and ritual - all these came under the strongest foreign influence in Moscow. In one form or another all public questions could be reduced to the one general question of borrowing from the West, and it was clear that those Russians who defended the old order were doomed to complete failure by the exigencies of practical life.

Russian historical studies provide much material for the study of Moscow's cultural borrowing in the seventeenth century and long ago rejected the old notion that Russian life was "immobile" and "fossilized" before Peter the Great. A complete exposition of the cultural evolution that occurred in the life of the Russian ruling circles during the seventeenth century would require many volumes. We cannot, of course, exhaust all the material that applies to our subject. We can select only the clearest and most characteristic of these data, in order to determine the material and ideological innovations that were adopted by the Russian people of the seventeenth century. We can present only the several characteristics of society which are most indicative of the tendencies of that era.

Let us begin with the military sphere.

II The Revival of Peaceful Contacts with Foreigners During the Reign of Michael Feodorovich. Dutch and English Agents in Moscow

With the first signs that calm had returned to the Muscovite state, foreigners again reached out to Archangel after the many years of disorder. The Dutchman, Massa, whom we have mentioned more than once, waited in Archangel from 1612 for the moment when it would be possible to resume trading operations with Moscow. In the interim he looked after the contraband that crafty Dutch speculators were removing from the Dvina: "many thousands of furs, in casks labeled tallow or cod liver oil." Of course, incidental exploitation by these robbers of the Russian North could not replace regular trade with Russia by the "Lord States-General of the Netherlands." Upon the first news of the accession of Michael Feodorovich and in reply to his official salutation, the Netherlands hastened to make Massa its official agent and charged him to look after Dutch trade interests in Moscow.

Independently of Massa and even ahead of him, many other Dutch merchants on their own initiative attempted to gain private commercial privileges from the new Russian Tsar. The Tsar had not yet been able to return to the capital from Kostroma, where he had been named Tsar, when he was overtaken in Yaroslavl by Dutch traders with words of congratulation and requests for charters and passes to Moscow. And they gained their objective. "The sovereign gave them Moscow," and did indeed grant George van Klenk, Mark Fogler and other Dutchmen the same rights and privileges they had enjoyed before the devastation of Russia. Under these circumstances Dutch trade immediately revived in the Muscovite state and began to grow even more rapidly than before the Time of Troubles, while the government of the Netherlands, the "States-General," as it was termed in Moscow, continued diplomatic relations with Moscow with great attention and dexterity. The citizens of the Netherlands continued to use the road to Moscow, which they found "as lucrative as sailing to Spain" (that is, to America).

The English, like the Dutch, lost little time. They also attempted to profit from the Russian Time of Troubles and, because of the breakdown of governmental supervision during those troubled years, extracted from the Russian North all that they could (furs, cod liver oil, etc.). But they did not risk going to the center of the state, for they feared violence and disorder. During the years of the "devastation" of Russia in 1611 and 1612, operations of the English "Muscovy Company," which functioned on the coasts of the White Sea and on the Pechora, earned a dividend of as much as 90 per cent, clear evidence that exploitation of the northern regions of unhappy Muscovy was conducted on a large scale.

The English merchant, John Merrick, a person remarkable for his talents and fascinating for his attitudes toward life, waited for a long time in Kholmogory and Vologda to renew relations between the English and Moscow. He was the son of William Merrick, who had been sent from England as a commercial agent to Moscow in 1573.[1] With his father he had lived in the English dwelling in Moscow (on the Varvarka), learned Russian and in 1584 also became an agent, in Yaroslavl. Later, in 1592, he was appointed an agent in Moscow. In the words of N. N. Liubimenko, he "belonged to the new era of Anglo-Russian relations, when the English deeply penetrated Russian life." Of the Englishmen who lived in Moscow during his time "many of the younger generation had been born and reared in Russia, knew the Russian language and were sent by their parents to England only for their education." When, therefore, they returned to Moscow for commercial work, they "acted not as newcomers in Russian surroundings, but just like natives."

Because of his personal abilities John Merrick was promoted from a simple agent of the English company that enjoyed the right of preferential trade with Russia to the ranks of its full and equal members. Afterwards he became one of its directors. During the reign of Boris Godunov he was in Moscow as an envoy of Queen Elizabeth, in 1602. He also played an official role at the time of the first Pretender. Afterward, when the Muscovite state completely disintegrated, he returned to England and there suggested the plan to establish an English political protectorate over the Russian North. For this purpose he was sent to Archangel by King James I, as we have seen above. When he arrived there in June, 1613 and learned that there was a new Tsar, Michael Feodorovich, in Moscow, he abandoned the idea of the protectorate, gave thought to the possibility of the consolidation of order in Russia and of reviving commercial relations with Moscow. He then returned to England, without visiting Moscow itself. The next year he appeared in Moscow entrusted with special powers and, in his role as political consultant and intermediary, engaged in lengthy negotiations with the Swedes. His adroit and intelligent work strengthened the position of the English in the Muscovite state and made it possible for them to return to Russian markets in great numbers and to retain their former privileges and advantages.

Thanks to the successes of the resourceful and talented Merrick, the rivalry of the English and the Dutch at the Russian court led at first to the triumph of the English. But this was ruined by the amazing tactlessness of Merrick's successor, the English ambassador to Tsar Michael, Dudley Digges. Digges was sent to Russia in 1618 with money from English trading organizations that had decided to grant the Muscovite government a large loan (perhaps as much as 100,000 rubles), on the condition that the Dutch be barred from internal Russian markets and that the Volga route be opened to the English for trade with Persia.

Digges arrived in Kholmogory in August, 1618, but there (probably after learning of the King of Poland's invasion launched against Moscow) he became frightened by the prospect of losing the money and quickly returned home. His flight by ship was to have been completely secret, but he set out to sea with much noise. Lest anyone take it into his head to detain him, he set out with his two ships "firing shots on all sides." He had so hurried that he left in the hands of his secretary part of the money he had brought. The Englishmen whom he deserted in Kholmogory (who also had some of the money) were brought to Moscow, where the Russians did not hide their indignation at Digges' action and ostentatiously flattered the Dutch, who arrived in Moscow at the same time with a "subsidy" from their country to the Tsar. This subsidy consisted of rather large amounts of gunpowder, lead, wicks and cannon balls.

From this moment the luck of the English began to change. The Dutch began to achieve greater and greater preponderance on Russian soil and the number of Dutch ships coming to Archangel began continually, year after year, to surpass the number of English ships. Undoubtedly, the causes of the decline of English trade with Russia lay also in the sphere of English political life of that time: English internal troubles were reflected in the course of England's foreign relations.

III The Influx of Foreign Traders and Military Men into the Muscovite State and Moscow. Regular Foreign Regiments

In this manner organized trade between European countries and Russia was restored after the Time of Troubles. At the same time there was also a spontaneous influx of foreigners into Moscow, once it had returned to peace. We have already seen that in the very first moments of Michael's reign the Dutchmen George van Klenk and Mark Fogler had personally solicited of him charters for privileged trade. In like manner the Englishmen T. Smith and "the knight Jonathan Ankin" somewhat later received the right of free trade not only in the *gostinye dvory,* but even in their own dwellings. It was customary for Moscow to ask the voevoda of Archangel why a certain foreigner had come on one ship or another. "Did he come in our name, or to serve as a hireling?" Apparently those who came "in the royal name," that is, for permanent service, were preferred and were summoned to Moscow. "But if any foreigner replies that he has come to serve us in hire," the voevoda was ordered to reply that " we no longer need people for hire, nor does our great sovereign." The voevoda was then instructed to "send him back to his own land," but to do so graciously. In the summer of 1613 the Englishman William Watts was treated in this manner. Pozharsky likewise treated Floderan's company, when it sought to be "hired out" to the popular militia that was moving to liberate Moscow. But when one member of this company of adventurers, Colonel Aston, reappeared in Russia in 1615 with a recommendation from King James I and desired to enter upon "service," he was accepted for such service. He was given the title of "Prince Arthur Aston, who has left the English land" and was immediately sent "to march against Lisowski," the well-known Polish partisan,[2] at the head of about 250 foreign mercenaries.

During these years the Muscovite government markedly desired to attract to Moscow even more foreigners who might wish to live in Russia. From one episode in 1614 concerning "trade with the Dutch lands by Simanka Klementiev, the son of Bus," we learn that Simon Bus was told in Kholmogory that "according to an imperial decree, we

First Half of the Seventeenth Century

have been ordered to send all foreigners from the town of Archangel to the sovereign at Moscow." Bus requested that he be left in the North, for he felt very much at home there and had traded there "for ten years and had purchased a house in Kholmogory and had married three years ago." It would be very inconvenient for him if "a foreigner such as myself, with his wife and children and all his animals, were sent to live with you, Sovereign, in Moscow." Bus was left in peace. But others were settled in Moscow, and not in the old manner, in special settlements, but throughout the entire town, with the exception of the citadels of the Kremlin and the Kitaigorod.

At the time of the approach of the Polish army of Prince Wladyslaw to Moscow in 1618, the "old" foreigners and those who were newcomers already constituted an appreciable element in the garrison of Moscow and were distributed, at times of attack, throughout various sections of the fortress wall in Moscow, along with the rest of the population. In later years (1620-40) the number of foreigners who lived in special dwellings in Moscow rapidly increased. "The Pokrovskaia section," D. V. Tsvetaev says, "remained their major center, but now they also appeared in the Tverskaia, Arbatskaia and Sivtsevy Vrazhok sections. On the eastern outskirts of the town two entire little villages sprang up. In Ogorodniki there was a 'German settlement,' which was small and a bit like a graveyard, and also a 'foreign settlement' beyond the old wooden town, on a line between the settlements of Syromiatnaia and Melnishnaia, which in 1638 had about fifty homes."[3]

In the middle of the seventeenth century the learned German from Holstein, Olearius (Adam Oelschläger), visited Moscow and counted as many as 1,000 men *(bey tausend Häupter),* Lutherans and Calvinists, serving and trading in Moscow. The number of foreigners in Moscow sharply increased when the government decided to recruit abroad entire regiments of foreigners and to form in Russia regiments on the foreign pattern composed of Russians. In 1630-31 a decree was issued to "give over" to foreigners serving in various towns "the children of landless *deti boiarskie"* and to "let them learn military matters in Moscow with the Muscovite Germans and from the two German colonels, Alexander Leslie and Franz Penzner, each of whom should take a thousand men." Then a decision was reached, in view of possible war with the Polish

Commonwealth, to send trusted people abroad to hire mercenaries. This same Alexander Leslie was ordered to go to Sweden and hire "five thousand willing foot soldiers." The lieutenant-colonel from Holstein, Heinrich von Dam, was sent to Hamburg and Lübeck with the same objective. He was directed to form and hire in northern Germany an entire regiment of 1,600 men. As a result, there flowed into Moscow many foreign newcomers, upon whom the population of Moscow looked with displeasure. Later we shall see how the Russians gradually removed all foreigners in general from where they had settled inside Moscow to special settlements in its environs. This took place in the 1640's.

All these "new arrivals" consisted almost entirely of representatives of various Protestant beliefs. Russia did not wish to have Catholics, and Leslie had been ordered to "hire military men who are good and true, but not to hire Frenchmen or others of the Papist faith." Catholic foreigners in Moscow were very few in number and could be found chiefly among those who happened to remain prisoner in Russia after the Time of Troubles or who simply became accustomed to this new homeland. But under Tsar Michael the struggle against Catholicism, which had been so bitter during the years of the Pretender and the Polish occupation, seemed to subside. The prime concern became that of defending Orthodoxy against the Protestant "heresies," which had been introduced by the mass influx of foreign merchants, soldiers and craftsmen of every type.

IV Orthodox Newcomers From the East and the Ukraine

We should also mention that people of other nationalities and faiths were moving into Moscow from abroad at the same time as the "Germans." Besides those who chanced to come from the Balkan peninsula for service in the army (and who were called in Moscow "Greeks, Serbs, Voloshane, Ugriane and Multiane" [Wallachians, Hungarians and Moldavians], during the first half of the seventeenth century clergy of various orders from the Orthodox East, from

First Half of the Seventeenth Century

patriarchs to simple monks, were continually appearing in Moscow. As time passed, they increased in number until the Muscovite authorities began to undertake prohibitive measures against their entry. Some of these visitors came only for a brief time, seeking "alms," that is, subsidies for their dioceses or monasteries and donations for themselves. But some of them came "in the sovereign's name," that is, "to live eternally away from the persecution of the Turkish people." These were received cordially but were helped generously only for a time. Those who had come "in the Tsar's name" were assigned to the work of "correcting books," in other words, to editorial work in the *Pechatnyi dvor,* and to the instruction of Russian youths in Greek and Latin for the same type of work. Those who begged alms were favorably received, then were sent home with rich gifts.

The day-to-day mode of life of these visitors was much more mundane than their officious demeanor indicated. Oppressed by the violence of the Moslems and suffering for their faith, Eastern bishops seeking the moral and material support of Moscow arrived at the Russian border with large suites that were often motley and strange in their composition. These retinues included every kind of rogue, often disguised as priests and monks, while merchants disguised themselves as servants. The Greeks themselves have written, for example, that the Patriarch of Jerusalem, Paisios, while en route to the Muscovite state (in about 1648-49) attached to his retinue anyone he encountered and enrolled them all as ecclesiastics, with the provision that they give him a certain part of the gifts they received in Moscow. In addition, he also enrolled in his retinue many Greek merchants, in order to conduct them and their wares to Moscow with public transportation and food and without inspection and customs. For this, it seems, he received a large bribe. One can imagine what people of various races and character arrived in Moscow as part of these pious caravans from the East and with what suspicion and mistrust Muscovites must have regarded these representatives of Greek Orthodoxy.

Those who came to Moscow from the Western Russian lands of the Polish Commonwealth were at first regarded with similar distrust. They greatly increased in numbers after about 1620. During the Time of Troubles many Lithuanian and Polish enemies of Muscovite Russia had invaded the country from there. After the Time of Troubles it was difficult for the Russians to determine which of those from Lithuania and Poland were Orthodox and which were Uniate, Catholic or sectarian, just as it was difficult to learn who was a true friend and who was a cunning dissembler or an overt enemy. The diversity of nationalities and differences in faith were extraordinary in the Polish Commonwealth, and for this reason, after Russia recovered its internal peace, Moscow had to examine closely the people who were coming from there "in the Tsar's name," in order to determine exactly their attitudes toward her. This also explains why the Muscovite authorities during the first period of cultural contact with Western Russians went so far as to "rebaptize" those who had already been baptized and tried to learn from everyone who came from there whether they "had been baptized with the Russian baptism, with three immersions," or whether water had merely "been poured on them from a little pitcher."

But time was to tell. Moscow valued the learning of her brethren in faith from Kiev and understood that she had to import Orthodox theological scholarship to Moscow. From 1648 the Muscovite government began to summon a number of learned Kievan monks and recognized their authority in questions of dogma and ecclesiastical organization. By the middle of the seventeenth century entire communities of Ukrainian monks had been organized in various monasteries in Russia. Thus as many as a hundred men who had come from various Ukrainian cloisters were assembled in the Dudin Monastery on the Oka River. Several dozen South Russian and Western Russian "teachers" were settled in the St. Andrew Monastery in the environs of Moscow. For this reason the monastery was known as "the special foreign monastery." Communities such as these were the main breeding ground of South Russian influence upon Muscovite society.

V The Attitude of Russian Society Toward Cultural Borrowing. The First "Innovators": The Opportunists (I. T. Gramotin) and Those Who Sought Truth (Prince I. A. Khvorostinin)

Such was the complex cultural situation in which the ordinary Russian found himself in the large centers of Russia, such as Moscow itself, Yaroslavl, Vologda and Novgorod. The foreigner who had come for service, the "German" merchant, the foreign technician who was an "expert" in one or another line of work, the learned Ukrainian monk, the Greek beggar covered by his sacred cassock, the Polish or Czech sectarian who felt it possible to base faith upon reason - all these types flashed before the eyes of the Muscovites, startled their imagination, awakened their reflection and disturbed their consciences with problems of life, the soul and faith. Russians who were more thoughtful or impressionable quickly responded to the innovations that these newcomers introduced either by beginning to sympathize with them and following them, or by beginning to seek ways to struggle against this imminent danger, in which they sensed the destruction of ancient principles.

As far as we can judge, opportunists and careerists predominated among those who sympathized with the newcomers. When the Pretender opened the gates of the Russian court to the Poles and their customs, imitators of "the Polish style" immediately appeared. When the Poles later captured Moscow and Pan Gosiewski began to rule it, not a few of these imitators gathered about him. Typical of these was the *diak,* Ivan Tarasievich Gramotin.[4] He had grown accustomed to the Poles and mastered their language in Tushino, at the time of the second Pretender. In the days of Gosiewski, Gramotin became "a gracious pan" and was very influential in the Polish administration of Moscow. His intimacy with the Poles was also promoted by the fact that during his youth he had twice gone to Germany, attached to embassies as a simple clerk. He had also visited the Czech lands, Hamburg, Lübeck, Leipzig, Dresden, Nuremberg and other cities.

Massa, who conducted business negotiations with Gramotin, knew all this and had this opinion of him: "He had been an ambassador to the

Roman Emperor, looked like a native German, was intelligent and reasonable in all things and had learned much while a captive of the Poles and Prussians." It should be noted that this "captivity" of Gramotin was not a military imprisonment, but, so to speak, a spiritual and voluntary one. He imitated foreigners and adopted German customs and the Polish language without compulsion. His intimate letters to important Poles in 1610 - 11 speak of how he openly supported Sigismund against Muscovy and was a traitor to his homeland.[5] But when circumstances changed and his homeland overthrew the Polish dictatorship, Gramotin knew how to become a patriot. He returned to Moscow from the Polish camp and there made a career for himself as a man of talent and experience. For many years (until 1635) he concerned himself with business and lived to a ripe old age. In all of Gramotin's actions one thing is always apparent - his desire for success in life - which he sought at the expense of his dignity and honor. There was in him nothing that was lofty or principled. For him foreign innovation was a convenient and welcome means to an end. The old principles had no value for him.

But alongside these practical men there were also men of conscience in Russia, men for whom the innovations which life had brought caused emotional anguish. Fate has happily preserved for us an image of one of these men. In the documents of the beginning of the seventeenth century, which are generally poor in biographical material, there are data for a study of the life and character of one of the most interesting figures of the Time of Troubles and the reign of Michael. We refer to Prince Ivan Andreevich Khvorostinin, who began his service at the time of the first Pretender and died in 1625. We can call him the first swallow of Russia's cultural spring, and one that suffered bitterly from the cold breezes of Russia's stagnation.

As a young man Khvorostinin was, like all aristocratic Muscovites, received into court service and was caught in the slime of debauchery and depravity in which the court of the first Pretender had wallowed. The Pretender included him in the closest circle of his reprehensible favorites and honored him with the title of cup-bearer [kravchii].[6] Khvorostinin greatly distinguished himself in his role as favorite and in his conduct. Foreigners clearly noticed him. Massa calls him a haughty youngster who permitted himself everything. The Pole, Niemojewski, describing the gala feast that followed the Pretender's wedding, recounts in detail how "after the first course, Khvorostinin, the cup-bearer of the great Tsar, a handsome youth of eighteen, though not tall," changed his clothing to another brocade caftan *(giermaczek)* - something that he did twice in the course of the dinner - and brought the Pretender wine in a beautiful goblet of mountain crystal. Khvorostinin's role at the feast, according to Niemojewski, was especially noteworthy, for he alone carried out two responsibilities before the pampered Tsar, that of carver and cup-bearer *(podczaszego).*

With the fall of the Pretender, Khvorostinin had to suffer for these things. He was sent to repent ("submitted to the rule") at the Monastery of Joseph of Volokolamsk. The reason for his banishment was explained thus: "Because you were close to the Pretender, and fell into heresy, and wavered in your faith, and profaned your Orthodox faith, and did not observe the fasts and Christian customs." At the Pretender's court, of course, it had been difficult to observe "Christian" (that is, old Muscovite) customs. But probably Khvorostinin's "heresy" was seen only in this, for at the time no other heresy, specifically against the church, was detected in him.

Shuisky's reign passed, and in 1610-11 Khvorostinin was again in and around Moscow. With other patriots he besieged the Polish detachment occupying Moscow. After the Kremlin surrendered to Pozharsky's troops, he was one of the first to enter the Kremlin to look for the grave of Hermogen, whom he respected as a most true son of the church and an ardent zealot.[7] In his historical work, "Accounts of the Days and Tsars and Saints of Moscow" *[Slovesa dnei i tsarei i sviatitelei moskovskikh],* Khvorostinin pathetically describes how, with other admirers of the Patriarch Hermogen, he asked a monk of the Chudov Monastery where they had buried the Patriarch. "Say where you have hidden from the heretics our teacher, who has suffered for Christ's sake . . . . Where can we find the body of the warrior and defender of the faith, tell us!" In his exclamations he clearly desires to appear an adherent of Orthodoxy who is far from any heresy. And apparently the authorities believed in Khvorostinin's rehabilitation from heresy. During the first years of the reign of Michael Feodorovich he was given responsible assignments. He participated in the wars with the Poles and was decorated for bravery and loyalty. His questionable past was, as it were, forgotten.

But after several years it was again recalled. When Khvorostinin no longer served on campaigns and marches but participated in court service in Moscow itself, his conduct aroused the suspicion of the authorities and elicited censure from private parties. Prince Semen I. Shakhovskoi, the well known writer of the seventeenth century, who, like Khvorostinin, came from the same family as the princes of Yaroslavl, knew Khvorostinin personally and has left interesting opinions of him in his works written about 1622. At that time Shakhovskoi had fallen under the Tsar's disfavor; even strangers extended to him sympathy and assistance, but Khvorostinin, his distant relative, not only failed to help him but did not even visit him. And meanwhile Khvorostinin, in Shakhovskoi's words, considered himself a man of moral perfection and even desired to preach to others. Shakhovskoi bitterly remarks of him that "such a man is in truth farther from morality than the haughty Pharisee is from humility." Afterwards Shakhovskoi wrote a letter to Khvorostinin, trying to persuade him to show his love and pity in this instance for those who suffer.

Later, when Shakhovskoi was a guest at Khvorostinin's, an interesting quarrel arose between them, which Shakhovskoi describes. The matter concerned the Sixth Ecumenical Council. Khvorostinin had said that it was not ecumenical and argued very boldly with Shakhovskoi. "Yesterday in his home," Shakhovskoi later wrote, "he reproached me and called me names before his servants, exalting himself in many ways and priding himself, I say, like a Pharisee. He feels that he surpasses all men in his knowledge of God's teaching and dogma. And he rudely and senselessly assaulted our teachings as being foreign to the tenets of the Holy Scriptures and the Fathers of the Church. And for some small remark that I made he scolded me angrily and fiercely."

Rebuking Khvorostinin for his rudeness, Shakhovskoi accused him of failing to recognize that "it is not wholesome for a man of faith to allow himself to be overcome by vanity or to act like a beast toward another." According to Shakhovskoi, he was not the only one to suffer from Khvorostinin's great cleverness, vanity and pride. "From his youth he was accustomed to acting with such arrogance," he says of Khvorostinin, corroborating with these words the earlier testimony of Massa concerning the behavior of the "haughty youngster who permits himself everything." Shakhovskoi was also able to observe the foreign influence upon his kinsman. He says that the main inspiration of Khvorostinin's errors and passions was a certain Zablocki, evidently a Pole, who had just converted to Orthodoxy.

The influence that foreign lands and foreign faiths had upon Khvorostinin was also noticed by the Muscovite government. Twice Khvorostinin's home was searched, and Latin books and images were discovered. It is generally known that he "was beginning to adhere to Latin and Polish priests and was associated with them." He was forgiven the first time. But Khvorostinin did not change his ways and began to deviate not only from Orthodoxy but from the general teachings of the church. He began to deny the resurrection of the dead and the necessity of prayers and fasts. He did not send his servants to church and during Holy Week in 1622 he "drank without end," ate meat, failed to attend church on Easter and did not go to the palace with greetings.

On the other hand, Khvorostinin also manifested a "vacillation toward treason." He thought "to leave for Lithuania," and it was suspected that this is why he petitioned the Appointments Bureau *[Razriadnyi prikaz]* to let him attend an ambassadorial conference on the Lithuanian border, instead of rendering "border duty" against the Nogai Tatars. Moscow seemed boring to Khvorostinin. "All the people are stupid and have no reason for living," he said. Russians "sow the earth with rye, but live a complete lie" *[seiut zemliu rozh'iu, a zhivut vse lozh'iu]*. He gave vent to his ennui and contempt for the Russian people in his writing. His rhymed works are little more than "many reproachful words written in verse" against Russian institutions. All this served as the pretext for Khvorostinin's banishment a second time, this time under the rule of the Kirillov Monastery.

He was sent there in 1623 and had to live in a special cell, under the supervision of a "good" and "strict living" old man. He was forbidden to leave the monastery, and no one could visit him. The Patriarch demanded that "he should not pass one day without observing the monastic rule, and should never miss church services." Prince Khvorostinin probably displayed signs of repentance quickly, for at the end of 1623 the authorities of the Kirillov Monastery, without asking the Patriarch, admitted their prisoner to confession and the Eucharist. For this they were censured by the Patriarch; yet at the same time the Patriarch himself felt it possible to forgive Khvorostinin the punishment that had been imposed on him. In November of 1623 he sent to the monastery "a scroll of instructions," which included a refutation of Khvorostinin's main error, concerning the resurrection of the dead. The authorities of the monastery first had to read it to Khvorostinin at a *sobor,* then demand his solemn renunciation of his former heresy. He also had to sign the scroll of instruction with his own hand. All this was done. The prince "was examined in the faith and gave his promise and oath" that he would strictly observe Orthodoxy. After this, on January 11, 1624, Prince Khvorostinin's servant, Ivan Mikhailov, brought to the Kirillov Monastery a letter from the Tsar that confirmed Khvorostinin's release from the monastery. The authorities were to send him to Moscow in their own carts and with their own lay brothers "caring for him and driving him." But the prince was sent like a convict, in the company of *pristavy* who were to inform the government in advance when he drew near to Moscow.

In addition to the letter to the authorities of the monastery, a second was sent to Khvorostinin himself. Here the sovereign and the Patriarch announced to the prince their complete forgiveness and offered him "to come look your sovereign in the eyes and be among his nobles as before." But Khvorostinin did not enjoy the favor of the sovereign for long. After one year, on February 28, 1625, he died and was buried in the Trinity-St. Sergius Monastery. At the end of his life he became a monk, taking the name Joseph.

Such was the life of Prince Khvorostinin. It is a rare personality of his century that can be characterized so definitely as he. His contemporaries agree remarkably in their moral assessment of him and consider him opinionated, haughty and insolent. Shakhovskoi, as we have seen, said this to his face. Government letters addressed to him declare the same thing. "You have thought that in intelligence no one comes within a mile of you," Moscow wrote him at the time of his release from the monastery.

We ourselves have the opportunity to be convinced of the truth of these opinions. Contrary to the literary custom of the time, Khvorostinin in his work, "Accounts of the Days," was far from modesty and self-abasement. In reporting his conversation with Hermogen, Khvorostinin does not hesitate to place his own praise on Hermogen's lips. He was so conscious of his superiority to other Russians that he could not concede to them or get along with them. He sought another milieu and, having tasted Polish civilization under the Pretender, strove for it afterwards. He read Polish books, associated with visiting Poles and prayed before Catholic icons. Having once ventured outside the complex of ideas accepted in Russia, he later went far in his denial and began to regard with scepticism even particulars of general Christian dogma.

But the boldness of his mind brought him little moral stability. If his early sins can be excused by youth, his later behavior openly testifies to his lack of moral discipline. A weakness for wine was Khvorostinin's main defect. The Patriarch, admonishing him to refrain from heresy, frankly told him that he was being ruined by "boundless drunkenness." When we read Khvorostinin's works we are also convinced that constancy of belief was not one of his virtues. Besides the above mentioned account of the Time of Troubles - "Accounts of the Days" - there has come down to us one more of Khvorostinin's works, his "Exposition against the Heretics" *[Izlozhenie na eretiki]*, a tract of complex structure that is set partly in prose and partly in syllabic verse. Its basic theme is the affirmation of "the Lord's teachings," that is, of Orthodoxy, with polemics against "heretics" - Catholics, Luther, Calvin, Servetus, Czechowicz and Budny.[8]

The reader who is familiar with this tract and knows the biography of its author cannot help but wonder at the evident contradiction between what Khvorostinin did and what he said. From documents that deal with his case, it is apparent that Khvorostinin really did wander into heresy. "You yourself, Prince Ivan," says the letter sent him by the Tsar and the Patriarch, "by your many unseemly acts have announced your own guilt. You yourself have said that you honored the Roman manner of writing, as much as you honor Greek writings." Khvorostinin had forbidden his domestic servants to attend church "and said that prayer was of no use and that there will be no resurrection of the dead." It seems that these words by Khvorostinin were deemed his major and most terrible delusion. Russian theologians composed in answer to this terrible "heresy" the "scroll of instructions" ("On the Resurrection of the Dead - An Instruction to Ivan Khvorostinin Based on Divine Scripture"), a copy of which is preserved in the Russian Public Library, with Khvorostinin's signature indicating that he had heard it. "With his own hand Khvorostinin" certified that "he has promised and pledged himself" to uphold Orthodoxy firmly and to believe in the resurrection of the dead.

As we collect the meagre and indefinite allusions to the essence of Prince Ivan's heresy, we inevitably conclude that in the present instance he was attracted by the views of the Socinian sects that were very widespread in Poland and Lithuania at that time.[9] Thus he was attracted by the very teachings of Servetus, Budny and Czechowicz that he had been ready to expose and refute zealously at another time. It was precisely the Socinians who spread the notion that the resurrection of the dead would be spiritual, in which the body would not participate, and that Christ would confer eternal life only upon the elect, and this would consist of union with the Beatific Vision. Inasmuch as the Socinians denied all sacraments except the Eucharist and Baptism and interpreted even these in a manner different from what was customary in Russia, Khvorostinin's attitude, once he had been captivated by their heresy, had to be rejection of the public worship of Russia. Therefore he really did "forbid his servants to attend church" and to pray in the Russian manner. But when his freethinking caused him to be imprisoned in the monastery, he learned from this bitter experience the force of the maxim, "do not seek truth from an alien law" and was quick to return to the Muscovite "law."

Yet Khvorostinin (and this is very strange) did not consider himself guilty of heresy and tried to pass it off that his "servants" (that is, his household serfs) had slandered him, while he had always remained Orthodox. In his "Exposition against the Heretics" he says that he "had exposed heresy for a long time," but when

> I lifted up my hands to be saved
> Against a certain heretical teaching,
> And instead of ink I used tears,
> And for this I have been fettered in irons....

But Khvorostinin had always placed his hope in the "Searcher of Hearts." He "had never denied His law," and this not just from the time that he was fettered "in irons" (shackles). But he "was not used to the games played by the unlearned and could not learn their moral habits." Because of this he was persecuted by them:

> I have written much about heretics
> But it has caused me great suffering;
> And because of my writings many were exposed
> And took up arms against me, as though I were myself the heretic
> I was condemned as a heretic
> And their malice against me grew.

As far as we can understand Prince Ivan's allusions, he was brought to punishment because of the denunciation of his own servants ("their very nature is evil"). He says:

> But even my slaves acted like devils toward me
> And destroyed the recesses of my soul.
> They took from me my strength and my defense
> And committed slander against me.

Khvorostinin lets us know that he had been too humane, that he treated them "with kindness" and fed them "with my own bread." But they had repaid him with evil:

> The race of slaves is damned;
> Their perfidy is quick and superb!
> Do not pour gold before swine,
> Lest they defile it with their feet.

And here, having revealed to his readers his "kindness" and brotherly love, Khvorostinin cannot refrain from a lofty evaluation of himself. At the conclusion of his tract he says of his serfs:

> I am the one who is above them,
> Placed over my own traitors.
> I have been appointed their lord
> And am glorified by God more than they.

He is thus amazed that serfs are believed when they slander their lord, who is "glorified by God:"

> I wonder about those who believe them.

Thus Khvorostinin's excuses were confusedly concocted. He was not really a heretic, but had been accused of heresy. He was merely a victim of the "unlearned," who could not understand his Orthodox sophistication. These were calumniators and slaves, who failed to appreciate his humanity. But his excuses cannot make us forget the force of the official accusations, which were based upon Prince Ivan's own confession, or the private opinions his contemporaries had of him, or the signature of one who was accused of heresy in the "scroll of instruction," which Prince Ivan gave "in his own hand." It is clear that his spirit wandered from one faith to another in search of truth and learning and was not slavishly obedient to Muscovite traditions. To Khvorostinin's mind, these had simply resulted from "lack of learning," and in his eyes the "habits" of earlier Muscovite generations grew dim before the lustre of foreign enlightenment and the success it realized in freeing the mind from the shadows of ignorance.

Khvorostinin's self-esteem, insolence and rudeness jeopardized him before those who wished him ill or those whom he offended and gave them grounds for complaints against him and denunciations. The instability of his belief, his moral slackness and his faint-heartedness led him to alter his views often and to repent of his actions with facility, though hardly with sincerity. According to the Russian expression, he was an "inconstant" man, who all his life wavered from one side to the other without hope of finding contentment or settling upon anything. In his verses he had charged that Russians "sow the earth with rye, but live a complete lie." But we have seen that he himself was far from living always by the truth.

VI *Those Who Defended and Observed the Faith and Ancient Customs (Ivan Shevelev - Nasedka)*

After Khvorostinin and Gramotin, who are striking representatives of the two different kinds of cultural "turncoats" of their time, we could

First Half of the Seventeenth Century 71

also point out other examples of renegades from the old Muscovite way of life who are not as well known. An example of these was, in the words of the renowned traveler, Olearius, "the notable merchant of Russian Narva" (that is, Ivangorod), Philip. Olearius prefers not to mention his last name, for when Olearius printed his book on Russia, this merchant was still alive. In 1634 German travelers visited Philip in the course of a journey and talked cordially with him. Philip told them that he "attached no importance to icons," that he interpreted fasting in his own manner and not as did other Russians, who during fasts ate fish and drank mead and vodka. "I shall be saved," he said, "if I take nothing but water and bread and pray zealously." But his views of true Christianity Philip kept to himself and would not reveal to his compatriots, for "I have no vocation for that," nor did he wish to pass for a madman or heretic.

Quiet and careful religious freethinking of this sort was peculiar, it seems, not only to Philip. In a book of worship printed in 1647 there is an interesting official reference to the fact that in the first half of the seventeenth century petty deviations from old Muscovite customs (such as shaving the beard) were common: "Not only did simple folk embrace heresy, but the powerful as well." It is impossible not to believe that there were many people like Philip. The exceptional events of the Time of Troubles and the influx of foreigners influenced minds, created new conditions of life and inevitably brought Russians together with new people and new ideas. Through their service and commercial ties Russians had to live with foreigners and at times were even dependent upon them in their business. Under such circumstances minds were emancipated, morals were loosened, traditions and beliefs ceased to constrain speculation, and freethinking or "heresy" was born. People began to scorn the churches, icons, fasts, confession and communion, criticized their rulers and priests, adopted "German" dress and became accustomed to shaving their beards (in the old phrase, "scraping the snout"). Attributing all these phenomena to the influence of Protestant religious propaganda, those who defended the old Muscovite way of life perceived that war against Protestantism and its manifestations was an immediate and most important task.

This war started with a literary struggle. To begin with, Russian theologians called attention to the many ecclesiastical books that had circulated throughout the Muscovite state after having been printed in various Russian printing houses in the Polish Commonwealth. The devastation, fires and pillage of the years of the Time of Troubles had destroyed many of these books. Now there were not enough books in Russia. The Muscovite *Pechatnyi dvor,* working with seven printing presses, could not satisfy the need for books. It was necessary to obtain books from abroad, and the authorities did not hinder this enterprise until 1627.

That year, however, saw the appearance in Moscow of many copies of a book by a learned Lithuanian "preacher," Kirill Trankvillion-Stavrovetsky, "An Instructive Gospel, or Words for Sundays and Holidays." This book had already raised some doubts in its native Lithuania. Its author himself had said of this work that "the corrupt word from the tongue of a detractor, filled with lies and the poison of the serpent of hell, swept everywhere throughout the land of Russia." The book entered Russia. The Muscovite censor found it heretical, and the authorities ordered it burned, "so that heresy and confusion will not arise in the world." Moreover, the order was issued to proclaim to all the people that "henceforth no one should purchase either books from Lithuanian presses or manuscripts written there." But the authorities did not stop here. In 1628 an order was given that in all the churches of the entire state all "Lithuanian" ecclesiastical books should be registered and removed. They could be retained temporarily only in places where services could not be held without them or where "the church would be without singing." Lithuanian books were also confiscated from private individuals. It was hoped that by such decrees one of the routes by which heretical influences were penetrating Russia would be closed.

Simultaneously with external and police measures of this sort, the protectors of the old Muscovite principles found it necessary to struggle against heresies on their own merits, through theological polemics. It was correctly understood that the Polish Commonwealth, a land where Catholicism held sway, was no longer merely a source of influence exerted by the "Roman faith," but now also by the Protestant views that had developed there. For this reason Russian polemics were almost always directed not against "the Latins," but against "Lutherans and other heretics." Many tracts directed specifically against Protestant teachings appeared. We can even say that the entire range of creative literary work of Muscovite Russia during the first half of the seventeenth century is entirely exhausted by only two themes: descriptions and reflections of the Time of Troubles at the beginning of the century and, later, theological polemics. Dozens of works of the most diverse merit, some translated and original, others compiled and independent, were devoted to both subjects. Russia came to the defense of Orthodoxy with great energy and produced, along with some wretched and poorly enlightened dogmatists, a number of remarkable champions.

We shall not dwell upon a general survey of this type of polemical writing. We shall pass over those tracts that are very specialized in character and scholastic in method, such as the work by an anonymous author, "On the Icons and the Cross," which was translated from the Western Russian into the Muscovite dialect (in the 1620's). We shall not take time to become familiar with the details of the works of the high-born princes Ivan Mikhailovich Katyrev-Rostovsky or Ivan Andreevich Khvorostinin. The first produced an ordinary compilation that is devoid of merit, "On Iconoclasts and All Evil Heresies." The second included an extremely intricate and complex tract of a moralizing nature in his "Exposition against the Heretics," which was written in verse and began with an acrostic. From this acrostic the name of the author is learned, as well as the title of the work, itself pretentious and not very reliable. In dealing with religious polemics we shall dwell upon other figures who are more interesting and more admirable in their personal qualities, as well as being more important for their role in expanding religious and national consciousness.

The first of these, the priest Ioann Vasilievich Shevelev, is better known by the name Ivan Nasedka. During the Time of Troubles he had "trudged" as a beggar to the Trinity-St. Sergius Monastery, found food and shelter there, had fallen under the influence of the famous Archimandrite Dionisius, and had become one of the most distinguished disciples of Dionisius' "school" (of which we shall soon speak). Nasedka's work that is of interest to us now are his polemics against Protestantism, which began from the very moment that Nasedka was sent to Denmark as a part of a diplomatic mission, which had as its objective the betrothal of Tsar Michael Feodorovich to one of the nieces of King Christian IV.

It is difficult to say whether Father Ivan had been charged with some special commission. But we can be sure that he did not sit on his hands during this embassy. During the entire journey he became acquainted, through books and personal observations, with the ecclesiastical life and teachings of the Protestants and gained a clear understanding of their customs and of religious life in Denmark. Nasedka expressed this familiarity in his official account of the embassy, which he composed in the form of a polemical work ("A Statement to the Lutherans"). It is considered one of the most solid of its genre.

The "Statement" is essentially a collection. Nasedka begins with a translation of the anonymous tract, "On Icons," then offers a number of his own discourses on all matters of controversy with the Protestants. Not satisfied with theoretical considerations drawn from written material, he often launches into sarcastic observations of his own and writes malicious satire against those aspects of Protestant life that he had been able to see with his own eyes. He relies upon his special information to describe the Protestant churches in Copenhagen and in the suburban castle of Christianborg, where he had been especially scandalized by a "chamber" *[palata]* over the chapel of the edifice. King Christian IV loved these buildings, for which he had himself prepared the designs and sketches. He built them in the new Renaissance style and loved to boast of the intricate splendor of his buildings. The Russian ambassadors were invited to dinner in this new palace of Christianborg and after dinner were shown the entire palace, which was still not wholly completed. "And the king himself had built the mansion from his own conceptions and had consulted none of his experts."

In deference to its builder the Russian ambassadors gave an impassive opinion of the palace in their account to the Tsar and said, among other things, that in the palace "we went through a church that had a chamber above it, and the ceiling of the church was engraved with gilded stones." And that is all. But this "church with the chamber over it" had aroused Nasedka's indignation. In his "Statement" he wrote in verse that the king "had erected a chamber on the second floor, and below it were two temples of worship. Lutherans would call them two churches; but Russians would see them as two doors to Hell that had been opened by Luther. On the upper floor there is a table set in that chamber for lechery and drunkenness, and on the lower there is an altar. Many people are brought into that church to marvel at the king's cleverness. Righteous men ought not marvel at such madness."

Nasedka naturally was also disturbed that the rooms of the castle contained many secular paintings and sculptures. "Too many naked bodies were made of gold and silver, and the shame of lasciviousness was openly exposed in them." The secular character of all Protestant churches bothered Nasedka. Their churches were always open, so "every kind of animal could get into them." The people conducted themselves with too much freedom. During the singing some of them stand, some sit, others lean on their elbows. The King of Denmark had also placed in his churches many of the bloody weapons that had been taken in battle. It was customary for all Germans to show their glory in this manner. All sorts of wares were also sold in their churches.

Commonplace material of this sort, which the priest Ivan includes in his "Statement," enlivens the work and gives it color and realism. Its author is made to appear to be a man who has seen and thought many things. Nor is the author's theoretical grounding insignificant. He is not simply a plagiarist and compiler. Competent critics of his "Statement" who are not inclined toward banal glorification find that in his tract Nasedka "appears as an enlightened pastor of the Russian Church of the first quarter of the seventeenth century."[10] Not only is he intelligently conversant with the Protestant teachings that he opposes, but he is generally well read in theology. He is versed in the Old and New Testaments and knows the commentaries on them (such as the *Margariti,* the *Zlatostrui* and others)[11] that were circulating at the time in various collections. He knows the work of Dionisius the Areopagite, Athanasius the Great, Basil the Great and John of Damascus. He has read the lives of the saints and the Apocrypha. He has read secular works in translation, such as Flavius Josephus and other "wise men." In the person of Father Ivan Nasedka Russian theology reached its pinnacle. Where Nasedka obtained such an education and where he gained such a comparatively serious literary and polemical style we shall now consider.

VIII The Archimandrite Dionisius and His Importance in the Society of His Day

If Nasedka occupied first place among the polemists who were the practical warriors for the faith against the actions and suppositions of its enemies, then first place among the directors of this struggle and among the educators of popular consciousness unquestionably belongs to the most unique man of this era, Archimandrite Dionisius of the Trinity Monastery. His contemporaries esteemed him so highly that he was canonized less than twenty years after his death. In 1652 the name of Dionisius, who had died in 1633, already appeared in the calendar of those saints "for whom a feastday has been established in Russia and to whom prayers may be addressed."

One man who undoubtedly knew him personally and now prayed to his icon was the Patriarch's court officer [stol'nik], Ivan Ivanovich Urusov, who lived in the first half of the seventeenth century. Many of those who esteemed Dionisius wished to have an image (a "likeness" or "icon") of their great contemporary, and for this reason many "sketchers" (icon painters) gathered at his coffin to paint his face. One of these portraits, which Urusov converted into an icon with a silver mounting, has lasted to our day and is preserved, with Urusov's signature, in one of the churches of the town of Rzhev. Such extraordinary respect was not bestowed upon Dionisius for nothing. The following pages will show what an extraordinary, we might say central, role this humble monk played in the intellectual life of the Russian society of his time and how much he did to replace the stagnant mentality of earlier generations with new and more enlightened attitudes.

Dionisius first appears in documents as a "widower priest," David Feodorovich Zobninovsky. He was also called "Rzhevitin" for the place of his birth, for he was born in Rzhev. His youth was spent in the town of Staritsa, where his father was an elder of the *yamskaia sloboda*. According to this and other information about his childhood and youth we can conclude that he was of peasant or rural background and was able to become a priest in the settlement because he had learned to read and write. He early became a widower and, according to Muscovite custom, became a monk because according to the law of the time a priest who was a widower lost the right to offer services and instead became a deacon or sexton. From the start the young monk Dionisius (he had been tonsured about 1601-02, when he was near thirty years of age) was assigned to the Monastery of Staritsa, where in time he became its superior, or archimandrite. Afterwards, probably about the year 1607, Patriarch Hermogen summoned him to Moscow and kept him at his side for special assignments. This summons testifies that Dionisius' reputation was then already great. Under the Patriarch he achieved importance as an adviser in directing lofty matters concerning the church.

When the Trinity-St. Sergius Monastery was liberated from siege in 1610 and had to be restored to order and its former dignity, Dionisius was named archimandrite of the monastery and remained in that position until his death. In this appointment he achieved unusual fame, we might even say glory. His restoration of the monastery, his great philanthropy, his patriotic agitation for the liberation of Moscow from the Poles, his participation in the work of the Muscovite *Pechatnyi dvor,* his broad and enlightened influence upon many spheres of contemporary society - for all this Dionisius became famous. His lofty spiritual qualities and his uncommon force of intellect, combined with an extraordinary and rare force of character, were characteristics that attracted to Dionisius sensitive hearts and impressionable minds.

Dionisius was a man quite singular for his time. He oppressed no one and exhibited neither a desire for power nor great obstinacy. A monk who was master of the monastery that had been assigned him, a monk who was bookish and loved theological and secular learning, Dionisius seems to have lacked the desire and the ability to wield power or engage in strife. With a constant smile and a kind joke, with compassion and kindness toward all whom he met, the archimandrite of the Trinity Monastery was always ready to yield in an argument and to suffer wrongs and humiliation. Among his coarse contemporaries qualities such as these did not evoke respect and sympathy. Dionisius was called a "fool" and "an unlearned country priest" because self-assured pride and garrulous wisdom were alien to him. The good, merry and humble archimandrite came to be respected, loved and even adored only when his quiet, inner virtues and his wonderful spiritual strength were recognized. Around him he sowed good and cultivated love for abstract learning. His cell became a second home for many who lacked shelter. Many who sought learning regarded it as their first school. Such figures of the seventeenth century as Ivan Nasedka and Ivan Neronov "trudged" in need to Dionisius and left his cloister not only recuperated and restored but inspired for intellectual and social labors. The writer Simon Azarin was obliged to his "benefactor," Dionisius (in whose cell he lived and worked for a long time), for all the charm of his literary realism.

Traces of Dionisius' personal influence are clearly perceptible in every ecclesiastical and social cause of the middle of the seventeenth century and in every literary development of this time. Dionisius deserves to be recognized as the head and center of the intellectual movement of his day, which in its beginning phase, when its main themes were only being outlined, awakened many Russian minds to the principles of correcting books, the importance of the Greek cultural tradition to Moscow, the relationship of Russia to lands of other faiths and the like. Although he appeared insignificant in the eyes of his own uncultured countrymen, Dionisius was highly appreciated by foreign co-religionists who were more cultured. The Patriarch of Jerusalem, Theophanes, regarded Dionisius with special favor and respect and honored him with many distinctions, telling him that "with our blessing you are to be the first and the senior among the illustrious brethren you have in great Russia."

Such is the image we have of the monk who was the peaceful champion of the faith and of learning. Dionisius' social and political work began in 1611. The fall of Moscow found Dionisius at the head of the Trinity Monastery, which had been devastated by siege and had to be restored anew. The fire in Moscow of 1611 left the entire population of the city without shelter and put them to flight.[12] "All roads were filled with refugees going to the monastery," and Dionisius began extensive charitable work, devoting all the resources of the still unrecovered monastery to help the persecuted and the suffering. Dionisius' gentleness and goodness did not prevent him from displaying inexorable firmness and energy in this good cause, in which he enlisted all the brethren at the Trinity Monastery. The monastery continued this charity for all of 1611 and in later years, and all who witnessed it speak of it with warm enthusiasm.

At the same time Dionisius was needed for another endeavor. He turned his thoughts toward the liberation of Moscow from the Poles and from its internal troubles, and he dreamed of "brotherly love and the unity of all the world." Concerning this he sent letters to everyone from whom he could expect sympathy and cooperation. These letters recorded "the countless number of Dionisius' cares for the entire Muscovite state." Well composed by the skillful scribes of the Trinity Monastery, these letters circulated throughout the state and were read with deep feeling.

Dionisius' expectations were realized. The country was pacified, class warfare subsided and state power was consolidated in Moscow. The time came to correct the evils that had caused the Time of Troubles. It was considered necessary to provide the church and the reading public with ecclesiastical books. Many of them had perished during the Time of Troubles. As we have already seen, books from "Lithuanian" presses had been pressed into service and the Muscovite *Pechatnyi dvor* had started to work strenuously. But the "correctors" (editors and proof readers) of the *Pechatnyi dvor* were naturally troubled by the problem of finding original works to be printed. From which originals ("translations," as they were called at the time) should new editions of sacred and official texts be made?

At the time of the "Hundred Chapters" *[Stoglav]*[13] it was known that the copied books contained many errors. It was decreed that "erroneous and miscopied" books should not be retained in the churches and that they should be corrected immediately, while "whatever writers were writing books in the towns" should be commanded to write "from good translations." But in those days who could certify that any text was "a good translation?" In those days there were no official editions, and everyone had to rely on his own judgment to determine the truth of any text he read. Many were convinced that the older a book, the more correct it was, for it was closer to the source of sacred scripture. If a book had been written on parchment, this was a clear sign of its antiquity. Book lovers, therefore, valued books on parchment especially highly and used them to verify all others. Another way to test the veracity of a text was to compare several books and collate their contents. But because the books to be used for this purpose were selected by chance, and since there was no exact criterion for choosing one or another passage as the most correct, the entire work of collating was futile and useless, reminiscent of the vague decree on correction issued by the "Hundred Chapters." For reasons such as these many of the books released by the Muscovite *Pechatnyi dvor* contained dubious passages and clearly needed verification and correction. The editorial staff of the *Pechatnyi dvor* demanded that these changes be made.

This situation was well understood in the Trinity Monastery. There, under the influence of Dionisius, the task of studying the texts of ecclesiastical books was begun and many critical commentaries on editions printed in Moscow were prepared. When these commentaries were sent on to Moscow, the correctors of the *Pechatnyi dvor* invited the Trinity monks and priests, with Dionisius at their head, to the *dvor*. Thus Dionisius came to direct this work as editor-in-chief. This happened during the period of the interregnum in the Patriarchate (1616-18), when Moscow postponed the selection of a new Patriarch until the Tsar's father, Filaret Nikitich, returned from captivity in Poland to fill this position.[14] Direction of the church was temporarily committed to the hands of the insignificant Metropolitan Iona.

Having begun the matter, Dionisius introduced something new, so much so that it seemed to the other workers a radical innovation. He did not allow himself to be content with the previous methods of work, which had aimed at correcting slips of the pen and went no further than simple emendations of little competency. He sought the principles according to which he could restore the correct and exact text of books in keeping with the dogmatic tradition of Orthodoxy and the ancient literary tradition. His exceptional mind suggested to him that the criterion of the authenticity of the text of Russian books could be in the end only the text of the ancient *Greek* books, properly verified, and that verification could be achieved through critical comparison of many "translations," that is, specimens of one and the same book. Such were Dionisius' ideas about the method of his work.

The extent of his work he also fixed differently than the correctors who had labored before him. They had not gone beyond petty editorial corrections and simple alterations of the text. But Dionisius did not stop at correcting the content of a text that seemed incorrect or meaningless to him. He was even prepared to alter ecclesiastical ritual, once he became convinced that it was not canonical. Inasmuch as Dionisius did not know the Greek language, he naturally turned to Greek texts for information infrequently and only in the last resort, and was unable to do this himself, but relied upon others. Because he was a deeply faithful man and careful in matters of belief, he generally regarded changes in the ritual with extreme discretion. Nevertheless, his views and methods were received with great hostility by the *Pechatnyi dvor* and Metropolitan Iona. As a consequence, Dionisius and his students and friends, such as the monk Arseny Glukhoi and the priest Ivan Nasedka (whom we already know) were accused of "heresy" and were arrested and brought to trial.[15]

Their case dragged on for a year, until Filaret Nikitich arrived in Moscow from Poland. Immediately upon his elevation to the Patriarchate, he demanded a final review of the case. For eight straight hours Dionisius "stood and replied" to Filaret and the Patriarch of Jerusalem, Theophanes, who happened to be in Moscow at the time. He expressed to them his views, brilliantly displayed his superiority over his accusers and fully proved his innocence. The Greek hierarch was struck by his unusual intellectual qualities. He warmly supported Dionisius and his assistants in the work of correcting books, then ostentatiously offered Dionisius his favor and respect. Upon a later visit to the monastery he honored Dionisius before all the brethren with special praise and an extraordinary award, the white cowl.[16] It seems that the Patriarch keenly appreciated Dionisius' "Grecophilism" and valued the importance of this trend to the future life of the Muscovite church.

Dionisius was indeed the first of his time to state the conviction that for correcting books it was necessary to study the Greeks and their ecclesiastical tradition. He was an admirer of Maxim the Greek,[17] approved of his work, personally used his books and translations and rehabilitated his reputation at his monastery. After Maxim the Greek had died in 1556, "in the home of St. Sergius, the Miracle Worker (i. e., at the Trinity Monastery), the books of Maxim the Greek had been little loved," nor were the brothers there allowed to read them. But Dionisius introduced them into use once again, along with selected texts of the Greek Fathers of the Church.

He generally trained his brothers to respect the ancient Greek theological writings. "Because of the efforts of this marvelous Dionisius," his biographer says, "the way was cleared for everyone, regardless of age, to approach this source." Dionisius' broad personal erudition and fine intellect allowed him to accept that which others could not yet comprehend, the superiority of Greek culture. And if we can agree with A. N. Pypin that Maxim the Greek "was the first connecting link between old Russian writing and the western school of scholarship," then on the same grounds we can name Dionisius the second of these links. From his time until the reforms of Nikon the activities of the Muscovite *Pechatnyi dvor* increasingly reflected Dionisius' attitudes. Nikon, of course, in his own superficial Grecophilism, was a brilliant and intemperate follower of Dionisius.

VIII Dionisius' Students *(Ivan Neronov, Simon Azarin)*

But one can speak of Dionisius' "Grecophilism" only with the qualification that it applied to the special sphere of book correction and theological knowledge. In everything else Dionisius was a pure Muscovite. The old precepts and the notion that the Russian people were chosen by God lived on in his soul. He continued to believe that once temporary ecclesiastical and secular "imbalances" had been corrected, Russian life would be elevated to its former inner perfection and purity. Greek guidance in scholarship he conceived only as a means; his objective was to restore ancient Russian piety in its local, popular forms, precisely those whereby preceding generations of Russians "had pleased God."

This national-protective attitude was stressed by the famous schismatic teacher, Ivan Neronov, when fate brought him and Dionisius together. According to Neronov's own account, which is inserted in his biography, he had to leave his native village as a youth because he had quarreled there with a drunken and scandalous clergyman. Neronov had so sternly accused this priest of drunkenness that even his own father-in-law had opposed him, and Neronov had to save himself from the village by escaping during the night to the Trinity Monastery. There he was introduced to Dionisius and told him of his virtuous outburst against the weaknesses of a fellow countryman. Dionisius became interested in the youth and "enjoined him to stay with him in his cell;" in other words, he included him in the circle of his pupils, of whom he always had many. "And Ivan (Neronov) lived not for a little while in the cell with the saintly archimandrite," until Dionisius was convinced that the youth whom he had sheltered "was true and faithful in all things." Then he sent him with a letter to the Patriarch, Filaret; and from this moment Neronov began his work, in the spirit of the principles with which Dionisius had inspired him.

Neronov was consecrated a priest and lived at first in his own village, then in the village of Lyskovo near Nizhnii Novgorod, then in Nizhnii itself. Everywhere he championed and worked for the renewal of the church and was an enemy of worldly banality and drunken debauchery. But the unusual ardor of Neronov's nature did not suit him either for the educational work of the kindly Dionisius or the brilliant work carried on around the court by the self-restrained priest, Stefan Vonifatiev, in whose Moscow circle Neronov found himself.[18] More than once Neronov incurred punishment, even exile, but forever he argued and struggled until finally, embittered by the constant fight for his ideals, he turned to schism and became an open enemy of the established church. During this phase, of course, he strayed far from the path marked out for him by Dionisius and from the principles with which the latter had inspired him. But in his basic beliefs he was undoubtedly the spiritual son of the famous archimandrite. Dionisius, as we have seen, acknowledged the cultural superiority of the Greeks, but remained an adherent of old Russian piety. In the heat of his struggle with the Grecophile Nikon, Neronov also defended old Russian piety, but could not accommodate it in his mind to a proper attitude toward the Greeks.[19] The pupil proved to be more narrow-minded than his teacher, but he did not thereby cease being his pupil.

Among the other pupils of Dionisius who achieved renown, besides Ivan Nasedka, Arseny Glukhoi and Ivan Neronov, we must mention Simon Azarin. He came to the Trinity Monastery from the aristocratic boiars' court of the princes Mstislavsky and spent his entire life working at the monastery. He was the "builder" (administrator) of the provincial monasteries subordinated to the Trinity, was often sent on private missions of an administrative and economic nature, served in the capacity of treasurer of the Trinity Monastery and, in the end, ended his life as a steward of the monastery. He devoted his leisure to reading and literary work. After his death the monastery inherited his large library, which included Azarin's own works. He was an ardent admirer of Dionisius. He lived under the same roof and in close spiritual contact with him for about six years, and after Dionisius' death he composed his biography, with the collaboration of Ivan Nasedka.

Spiritually, Azarin was wholly Dionisius' creature, and in this respect he is of great interest to us. He was no theologian or theoretician. He was adept at practical work, management and administration. But in addition he was extremely well read and possessed a fine literary style. Moreover, he composed his works not in the trite forms of the artificial and verbose eloquence that was then so common, nor did he succumb to "meandering words." Rather, he offered his reader a simple and direct statement of his topic that can only be termed realistic. The historian V. O. Kliuchevsky, who is severe in his judgments, says of Azarin: "Simon looked upon the duties of the biographer much more strictly than did the majority of old Russians who composed lives of the saints. He is more discriminating in his use of sources and ensures that his biography is not only complete but factually exact." He seeks the truth diligently, because to his mind "God does not wish to be glorified with false words, and the saints object to being glorified with fanciful miracles." He is very careful to show the reader the source of his information, "to see and judge how it was," and is careful not to appropriate the work of another, "never to attribute to one's own mind the work of another." The simplicity and clarity of Azarin's exposition are combined with sincerity and serenity.

But in anything that deals with the defense of the faith and nationality, he is an implacable a fanatic as Neronov. To Azarin is attributed the "Tale of the Devastation of the Muscovite State" *[Povest' o razorenii Moskovskogo gosudarstva]*, which was among the manuscripts he left after his death. Written before the Polish War (1654-55) of Tsar Alexis Mikhailovich, this tale reveals the author's uncompromising hostility toward the Poles and his desire to avenge Polish brutalities during the Time of Troubles. The sharp feeling of ethnic hatred and national exclusiveness that lies at the basis of the "Tale" and which is usually alien to Azarin's gentle nature recalls Nasedka's keen polemical attitude and derives from the same source - the cell of the kindly Archimandrite Dionisius, from which each of his pupils carried away the precepts of his teacher in the form that his own nature could accept.

IX The Official Tendency (Prince S. I. Shakhovskoi)

Such were the leading figures of the orientation that sought to protect Muscovite ways. Under Dionisius' influence these polemists and representatives of national consciousness started from the point of view that Moscow was the Third Rome and was sinless and immutable at every moment of her existence and in every manifestation of her spirit. To their minds Russian life "had been made leprous" by the Time of Troubles and was no longer unstained. It had to be reformed and returned to the old principles, and therefore it was necessary to rely not only upon the national heritage but also upon the theological knowledge of the Orthodox East. At the same time it had to be protected against the possible influence of all sorts of heresies, "Latin and Lutheran," by banning and sternly opposing them.

This program was not only proclaimed in literary circles but was also accepted by the authorities. High official circles listened attentively to the opinions of learned Orthodox Greeks and Ukrainians whose orthodoxy was not suspect, while at the same time they brutally punished their own subjects, if they observed or even suspected them of "vacillation in faith" or the slightest deviation from the rules of the church. Ivan Neronov, who had been shown such great kindness by the Patriarch Filaret because of Dionisius' letter of recommendation and who had been ordained a priest because he was "true and faithful," later found himself in exile for a year in a monastery of the far North, because "he taught people without the Patriarchal blessing." "Because of his pride and haughty attitude" and the independence of his views, and because he "abused priests and called them heretics," he was thought to have "a mind frenzied from madness." It was resolved that he should learn monastic humility, until he returned to "perfect reason." The well-known amateur theologian and most Orthodox courtier, Prince Semen Ivanovich Shakhovskoi, suffered even more severely.

The fate of this devout prince was such that he found himself almost continually in disfavor, exile and even imprisonment, despite his devotion to the authorities, his zeal for the church and his love for theological reflection and writing. He was made to suffer for the crimes of other members of the Shakhovskoi family because the principle of group responsibility was adhered to in those days, even though he had not participated with them "in those offences." He also suffered because of his overly frequent marriages. Upon the deaths of his wives he hastened to marry for a third and even a fourth time.[20] Finally, he suffered because, though he was irreproachably Orthodox, he committed obvious breaches of tact in his theological statements. The apparent cause of all these misfortunes was Prince Semen's peculiar cast of mind, which did not allow him to appreciate people and events with sufficient quickness and understanding. Hence, he is a typical example of how the Muscovite authorities punished their own servants for even inadvertent transgressions against the faith and policies of the church. The disgrace that Prince Semen suffered because of religious matters deserves our attention.

In 1644 the Danish prince, Waldemar, came to Moscow to marry the Tsarevna Irina Mikhailovna. During the negotiations that preceded his arrival Russian diplomats had been firm on the point that the prince

First Half of the Seventeenth Century

had to accept Orthodoxy before he came to Moscow. But Waldemar, as well as the pastor who accompanied him, began to argue this point in Moscow. The prince was adamant in not wishing to change his faith. Moscow roused all her theologians, among whom was Prince Semen, and gave the debate an extremely serious atmosphere. Entire tracts were written and all sorts of inquiries were conducted during this debate between the Russian scribes and the pastor. Ivan Nasedka, whom we know, directed the enterprise. Prince Semen was also zealous in his participation.

When Waldemar's stubborness became known, one of the Russian theologians, a priest of the Cathedral of the Assumption named Nikita, had a discussion with Shakhovskoi. "We have come upon a problem," Nikita said, "and we have got to solve it." Shakhovskoi asked, "What problem is that?" Nikita explained: "The problem is that the prince does not wish to be baptized (into the Orthodox Church)." To this Shakhovskoi replied, "This problem can be solved by bringing the prince into the Church unbaptized."[21] And having expressed this bold idea, Prince Semen added that he had already prepared a letter to that end. But when the priest asked to see the letter, Prince Semen refused to give it to him. But the priest denounced him, and the letter was demanded and obtained from him. The upshot was that both collocutors suffered for their discourses. The priest was separated from those who were carrying on the debate with the pastor, while Prince Semen was removed from Moscow. The boiars who examined his letter[22] found that "he had become an adherent of the prince" and had, with his advisers (that is, the priest Nikita), intended to deny the Orthodox faith. Shakhovskoi was sent to a remote post in Kola, where he remained for two years. This severe punishment befell the prince merely because he had thought that perhaps Waldemar did not have to be baptized "with three immersions," and requested that he merely curse his "Papist" faith and accept the Russian creed, worship the icons and observe the fasts.

Prince Semen, though inoffensive by nature, suffered further severe punishment because of the religious rigor of the Russian authorities. When he returned to Moscow two years after his banishment, Shakhovskoi was sentenced to death for a single careless reminiscence of his ill-fated letter. When he was presented to the young sovereign, Alexis Mikhailovich, to justify himself for the affair of the letter, Prince Semen told the Tsar that "he had done all that in fulfilling an order of his father, the Sovereign of blessed memory." These words were, of course, imprudent. They seemed to shift responsibility for the "heretical" views to the dead sovereign. The Tsar ordered that Shakhovskoi be interrogated to learn exactly what had happened. He confessed that he had not expressed himself precisely and that "he had written the letter himself" and not on the Tsar's order. For this reason his case was reopened and once again he was accused of "heresy and great duplicity." It had been a long time since Prince Waldemar had been in Moscow, and the matter of his marriage was now forgotten, yet Prince Semen "was sentenced by the boiars to be burned," because he had "become an adherent of the prince." On January 4, 1647 his death sentence was read on the square before the *Posol'skii prikaz* in the Kremlin. But an announcement was then read that, through the mercy of the sovereign, the death penalty was commuted to exile in Sol'vychegodsk.

X Those Who Defended the Market: Russian Traders and Their Allies From Other Classes of Society

Thus official Moscow sternly and decisively defended the inviolability of the age-old principles of Russian life. Yet at the same time Russian life departed ever farther from those principles. In the middle of the seventeenth century, during the early years of the reign of Alexis Mikhailovich, the encroachment of the foreign element upon Russian life achieved great and obvious success. While heated arguments raged over ideas and faith and the policies of national preservation were strengthened in every possible way, in the realm of commerce and industry and in the military and technical fields a real turnabout was gradually completed.

Russian commerce finally fell into the hands of foreign capital. Foreign owners were now prepared to take into their own hands the processing on the spot of Russian raw materials. The Muscovite government became more and more accustomed to placing orders and making purchases through its own foreign agents. Masses of people of various nations were received into service in Moscow - military men, physicians and technicians. Moscow became filled with these foreigners, who bought homes for themselves in the central quarters of the city. The same could be observed in all other large cities. Foreigners who were in service received for that service *pomestie* in various districts and were settled on the land, with serf labor made available to them.

The Russian people, who were far from any ideological consideration when defending their own practical interests, had to experience in one way or another the real consequences this influx of foreigners had upon their way of life. Many of them, of course, handled the matter simply and tried to extract from this new situation the greatest possible benefit. They entered into dealings with the foreigners in order to profit from them. They supplied them with wares and hired themselves out to them as commercial agents or as simple servants. This caused no religious or cultural problem. But at times the problem of self-interest arose. Contact with foreigners in the fields of commerce and business generally led to the triumph of foreign capital and foreign ownership and destroyed Russian contractors and competitors. Contact with them in the realm of military service, where the foreigner was the instructor and commander, offended and eroded self-respect. Well before the crisis in Russian social life which became evident during Tsar Alexis' early years, the problem of the foreigners had been raised by the most diverse layers of Russian society, independently of higher ecclesiastical and governmental circles.

The Russian commercial class began to speak out earlier than all others. Very early (we can say immediately after the Time of Troubles) it had begun to show the Muscovite government its dissatisfaction with foreign commercial competition. Thus in 1620 the Russian *gosti* (merchants of the highest rank) declared that Russian merchants could not compete with the English, and that the English "never agree with us in anything," for "the English people are strong and rich." They were strong because of the privileges and advantages they had enjoyed since the sixteenth century, thanks to the kindness of the Muscovite government and the bribing of influential clerks in the *Posol'skii prikaz*.

And they were rich because they worked with organized corporate capital and possessed great experience and knowledge of the international market.

But during the third decade of the seventeenth century English trade in Russia began to slacken, and the English lost their superiority to the Dutch, who had begun to send to Archangel ten times the number of ships as the English. Understandably, the dissatisfaction of the Russian merchant class shifted from the English to the Dutch. They were especially struck by the grain operations of the Dutch in Russia. The Dutch controlled the grain market of all Europe and now counted on making Russia their main supplier. Dutch traders would provide the countries of Europe with Russian grain.

Not only did the Dutch openly buy up Russian grain wherever they could, they even exported it clandestinely. They found it necessary to do this because shipments abroad of grain from Archangel had become a state monopoly, which it was profitable to circumvent. In their complaints against the commercial tricks of the foreigners and especially the Dutch, the Russians showed that foreigners bought grain not only from the state but purchased it from private individuals in exchange for trifles. They commissioned their own stewards and Russian agents for these purchases and gave Russian merchants loans to obtain for them grain, which they poured into their storehouses and later sent to their ships. In Vologda alone in 1629 local authorities opened eleven of these illicit storehouses, which had been constructed for foreigners in the courts of monasteries and in private households.

But inasmuch as the state standardized grain operations in accordance with its own objectives, Russian merchants could not protest against them. To make up for this, they protested other features of foreign trade. In 1627 there was presented to the Tsar the first (to our knowledge) petition of the Russian merchant class against foreign traders. "The *gosti* and commercial people of Moscow, Kazan, Yaroslavl, Nizhnii Novgorod, Kostroma, Vologda and all the other towns of the state" humbly ask that "the Germans from Brabant, Holland and Hamburg, as well as the English merchants, no longer travel as of old from the towns of Archangel and Kholmogory to the rest of the territory of the state and no longer build their households in

Russia or establish their businesses as of old on the Russian shore of the Arctic Ocean and in Siberia."

The motives behind this petition were thoroughly expounded. In brief they were as follows. After the Time of Troubles ("since the devastation of Moscow") foreign merchants had spread throughout the Russian state. In the towns they began to buy "tracts of land from the people settled there" and to build on them their households. Here they kept their wares, avoiding the official warehouses *(gostinye dvory),* and did not declare all their wares for customs. In these dwellings they also carried on retail trade, thereby "taking trade away" from Russian merchants. "Now these Germans have their storehouses and shops in Vologda, Yaroslavl, and Moscow and sell all sorts of wares on their own." In addition, the Germans buy Russian salt at the mouths of the Dvina and transport it in their own vessels to the center of Russia, enriching themselves thereby and depriving Russians of business. With Russian goods purchased in Russia they began to trade among themselves even in Archangel, while "in the customs house they record that these wares are for passage" (that is, for export). Thus their commercial operations on Russian territory escape legal taxation, and "in this manner the sovereign loses his duties."

What is more, the Germans exploit the fact that the government allows foreigners to fish "in the Frozen Sea"[23] and secretly export grain from that region. Foreign ships enter the mouth of rivers seemingly "to fish and obtain tallow" (that is, to extract blubber oil), but in reality pour into their ships "all sorts of grain - rye and hemp and peas" - and export them abroad. Because of this, "grain is becoming dear" throughout the North and "all the places of the Pomorie are dying of hunger."

These details recreate for us a picture of the broad development of foreign commercial operations in Russia, because of which, in the opinion of Russian merchants, "great poverty had come upon them." To Russian merchants it seemed that the organization ("the agreement among themselves") of the foreign merchants was astonishing and improper. They adroitly "raised the price" of all Russian goods, informed their homeland of the state of the Russian market, received from their countries "missives" with instructions and, because "their knowledge of Russian goods" became so timely and precise, they "knew at what price they should buy Russian goods." And so, "they purchase Russian goods on orders, as in a conspiracy."

Of course, systematic and organized purchasing gave the foreigners the goods they most needed at a price that was the most profitable for them, while Russian merchants "found themselves without business because of these foreigners, and many trading people left their businesses and for this reason suffered want and incurred great debts." In view of all these circumstances Russian *gosti* and traders asked the government to bar the foreigners from internal Russian markets and stop their abuses in the havens of the North. Earlier, they said, foreign traders "had not been permitted" to trade beyond the harbors, "and in those days the sovereigns collected their duties, while we, your slaves and orphans, were great merchants. In those years we could serve in the service of Your Highness with gladness, and not with sorrowing."

This sort of petition was issued many times, in the years 1642, 1646 and 1648, each time with more and more detailed reports of the misdeeds of the foreigners. Russian commercial people stubbornly and persistently asked that foreign traders be barred from the interior of the country and that their "courts" be liquidated in the towns, where they "sat" with their wares, traded "on their own" and cornered Russian goods, "enslaving many poor and needy Russian people." Such requests and complaints led to complete investigations by the Muscovite authorities. Information was collected on bygone times, what sort of privileges had been extended and to which of the foreign merchants, and when. The petitioners were asked to express their own opinion of how foreign trade could be liquidated in Russian towns. "Would not the Muscovite state be disliked by foreign governments for doing this? And it should be kept in mind that the Russians owe some money to foreign merchants. It would not be possible for the Russians to pay these debts at once. And to whom would the Russians pay these debts, once the foreign merchants have departed? Besides, the foreigners have built storage places in Moscow and other cities and now there would not be any foreign merchants there. Whom would we pay for these storage places?"

To these disturbing questions the petitioners replied that they "would not expect the foreign governments to be displeased," because it would be important to the foreigners to continue trade with Russia even through the town of Archangel alone. As for the payment due the foreigners for their confiscated markets and the debts owed them by Russians, these "would peacefully be paid by the *gosti* and other merchants." If in some instances the foreigners did not have an official document to prove that a Russian owed them money, these cases would be "settled to the satisfaction of both parties." Consequently, the government felt it necessary to meet the desires of the Russian merchants at least half way and resorted to several restrictive measures. One of these measures firmly stated that "in Moscow and other towns foreigners will not sell retail goods, and if they do sell at retail, those goods should be confiscated by the Great Sovereign. And they should not come into fairs and towns with their goods and money, nor should they send their stewards."

Thus foreigners were forbidden to sell at retail and to corner markets. They were left with the right only to wholesale trade. They were forbidden to trade "among themselves" and "from foreigner to foreigner" on Russian territory, and were to trade only with Russian traders. But because of formal reasons and practical considerations the Russian government found it impossible to honor the request that foreign merchants be banned from the interior of the country. On the one hand, treaties were involved (such as the treaties of Tavzin and Stolbovo with the Swedes), according to which it had been agreed that foreign merchants had the right to trade not only at the docks and border towns but also in several internal markets of the Muscovite state. Secondly, the government itself maintained such great and complex commercial exchange with foreigners that it was of no mind to dismiss them from Moscow and other commercial centers. If we add that the Muscovite administration was not in the habit of punctiliously fulfilling the commands of its authorities, we can understand why foreign traders continued their tactics, despite all these prohibitions. They remained within the state, engaged in buying up Russian raw materials, traded among themselves, avoided customs inspections and sold their wares at retail. The solicitations of the Russian commercial people did not achieve their end.

This also explains why the *gosti* and other merchants turned for help and support to other groups of the Russian populace. The service people *[sluzhilnye liudi]* and clergy joined the opposition to foreigners simultaneously with the Russian traders and occasionally in collaboration with them. At the *zemskii sobor* of 1648-49 representatives of the middle classes, the nobility and the *posadskie liudi*, (notably the traders) apparently reached an agreement and constantly acted "as one." The service people presented petitions in support of the taxed people *[tiaglye liudi]*, while the petitions of the taxed people supported the service people. As a result, the government encountered purely class interests and found itself opposed by the entire people, by "all the land." Thus, on the question of removing the foreign merchants to Archangel, the petitioners were not merely *"gosti* and commercial people," but primarily "the palace officials and courtiers, the Moscow gentry and the nobility of other towns, as well as the *deti boiarskie"* (that is, all "ranks" or categories of the service class). While the matter was being discussed in detail, the government "interrogated" not only specialists in commercial affairs but also people of the noble "ranks," who offered their own opinions, together with those of the merchants.

Apart from this organized cooperation, which was handled in the proper manner, the mass of service people occasionally came out against the foreigners crudely and spontaneously. During the months that saw the problem of foreigners being debated in the *zemskii sobor,* a movement against foreign commanders developed in the armed forces. A Swedish resident in Moscow, Pommerening, reported to Sweden that 2,000 noble Russian cavalrymen no longer wished to be commanded by Dutch or other foreign officers, whom they termed unbaptized. The government then trained some 200 of these cavalrymen to train their fellows and command them.

The clergy joined its own attacks against the foreigners to those mounted by the service class. There has come down to us the story of how Patriarch Nikon at the beginning of his Patriarchate stirred up persecution of foreigners because they wore Russian dress in Moscow. This came about because once when Nikon participated in a large procession in the city and was giving his blessing to those standing about him, some foreigners who were among the Russians did not bless themselves and did not bow before the Patriarch, as the Orthodox did. Nikon became angry and insisted that henceforth foreigners be forbidden to wear Russian dress. "So nowadays," says Olearius, "all foreigners, of whatever land, have to go about in the dress of their own nation." Without disputing the veracity of this story, we can observe that Nikon inherited his hostility to foreigners living in Moscow from his predecessor, Patriarch Joseph. In Joseph's own time the Russian clergy began to issue admonitions against living with foreigners, and Joseph himself, as well as several boiars, wished to expel from Moscow not only foreign traders but also foreign officers living in the capital.

But such charges brought by individuals to the government were unsuccessful as long as full-scale movements against foreigners did not develop within the church. It was precisely through the initiative of sizable groups of the Russian clergy that foreigners in Moscow began to be limited in their rights and their places of residence. At the beginning of 1643 Russian clergymen from about ten parishes in the Miasnitskaia and Pokrovskaia sections of the city presented to the Tsar a petition that "in their parishes the Germans have established chapels in their courts near our churches, and the Germans keep Russian people among themselves in these courts, and the Russian people suffer every sort of sacrilege from these Germans. Because of these Germans the parishes are empty." The clergymen therefore asked that "the sovereign help them and order the Germans banished from these courts" and command that henceforth "Germans not purchase courts and homesites in these parishes." The sovereign complied with this petition only in part. He did not banish the foreigners but did decree that "the chapels that have been built by Germans in courts near Russian churches be pulled down," and that throughout Moscow "Germans and the widows of Germans are not to purchase courts or homesites from Russian people."

But ten years later the populace of Moscow tried to obtain what their clergy had not yet achieved, namely, complete eviction of foreigners beyond the limits of the Russian capital. This measure was occasioned by the great fires that ravaged Moscow in 1652. Afterwards, when the rebuilding and reorganization of the burned out quarters were being discussed, the question was also raised about allowing foreigners to construct a special place for themselves beyond the limits of Moscow and outside its "settlements" and "streets." From the fall of 1652 there began to arise the famous "new foreign settlement beyond the Pokrovka Gates and beyond the Zemlianoi Gorod *[Earthen City]* beside the river Yauza," that is, "they divided the land in that German settlement, measuring it out according to regulations."

Henceforth there was formed near Moscow that foreign settlement, the cultural influence of which proved, contrary to the expectations of those who defended the old Muscovite way of life, much stronger than had been the simple commingling of foreigners and Russians in the streets of Moscow.

Chapter Three

THE SECOND HALF OF THE SEVENTEENTH CENTURY

I   The Domestic Crisis in the Muscovite State in the Middle of the Seventeenth Century. General Significance

The events that we have recounted concerning Russia's relations with foreigners were paralleled by other processes of great importance to the internal life of Russian society. The Time of Troubles of the beginning of the seventeenth century gave rise to the independent activity of social groups that during the sixteenth century, before the Time of Troubles, had been passive material in the hands of the patrimonial Muscovite authorities. The need to provide for their own self-defense schooled the tax-paying communities of the towns and the northern rural districts in political activity. Not only did each of them manage its own military organization, but they learned how to form great unions of towns and districts for the struggle with hostile national and social forces. Their organization for tax-paying purposes, with its customary and age-old forms of communication and mutual guarantee, facilitated the transition to more complex forms of organization, while the fortification of towns gave them a certain steadfastness and power.

Crushing a town community by a simple military raid was impossible, and dispersing people who were densely settled in a permanent neighborhood was not easy. It was much easier to do this with the districts inhabited "by nobles and the *deti boiarskie,*" the service people who were individually scattered about their service estates and patrimonies and assembled into a "hundred" or a "town"[1] only upon notice from the government. The appearance of an enemy detachment (Lithuanian or Cossack) in such a district forced the gentry and the *deti boiarskie* either to scatter or to surrender to the enemy. Most often they fled behind the fortified defenses of the towns and there joined the town community. From it they received protection and their daily bread, and to it they contributed military leadership and at times even administrative experience. Since the conditions of life in their own class did not provide sufficient grounds for a class organization, the nobles were schooled in it by the example of the townspeople and the peasantry, with whom fate threw them together during the "devastation" of the state. The union of nobles and towns, which was formed in this manner in 1612, proved to be strong enough to liberate the country from its foreign enemies and to restore it to internal order.

The impressions and experiences of the Time of Troubles were not forgotten after the pacification of the country and the election of a new Tsar. The Tsarist authority that was restored in 1613 was not in essence the old patriarchal and patrimonial authority of the sixteenth century. It ruled the country with the assistance of representative assemblies, *sobory,* to which the service and tax-paying classes were summoned. At these assemblies the representatives of both classes learned to understand the situation facing the state, to determine and defend their own class interests and to make organized demands.

The procedures of these assemblies and old Muscovite custom provided the legal grounds for such demands. In the course of the assembly one or another class group would find a pretext to present in the Tsar's name an "account" (report), and in this "account" it would state its wishes in the form of a petition, which remained for the Tsar to satisfy. The same sort of petition was also composed outside the assemblies by people of various categories. We have already spoken in detail of the petitions directed against foreign trade by Russian merchants. We also know of more than a few similar collective community petitions based upon other pretexts. All of this demonstrates that the activism developed during the Time of Troubles was not lost by the populace and that it was consciously related to the surrounding political reality and attempted to influence it.

Second Half of the Seventeenth Century

By the end of the reign of Michael Feodorovich (1613-1645) the practice of collective appeals to the authorities had become permanently established. But at the same time we have proof that the government did not satisfy all the desires of the class groups. There is no need to explain here the reasons for this. Suffice it to say that when the service classes and the tax-paying classes did not receive the desired response to their solicitation, they expressed their dissatisfaction and displeasure. In the middle of the seventeenth century these expressions began to multiply at a very rapid rate and attentive contemporaries understood that the matter might come to a dreadful denouement.

Swedish diplomats who were in Moscow during the last years of the reign of Michael Feodorovich reported to their government that the Muscovite "state system is precarious, and an upheaval in the near future is inescapable," and that in Moscow "a general uprising will occur" soon. The Russian people themselves said that they saw "sadness in everything, and confusion was great." The difficult economic situation, the ascendancy of foreign capital in the markets, the burden of taxes, the dispersal of the working populace from urban communities and from the fields of landlords - all this disturbed the populace. At the same time unwise authorities made life even more burdensome by creating the general conviction that the ruling powers did not wish to help the people in their need, because they were under the influence of mercenary boiars. This is why the Russians expected the boiars "to be beaten from the land."

The change that occurred on the Muscovite throne in 1645 accelerated the crisis. With the accession of Alexis Mikhailovich (1645-1676) new people came to power and new hopes arose among the populace. But these new people brought with them no change for the better. Then a series of disorders occurred in the state. In 1648 a wave of revolts spread from Sol'vychegodsk and Velikii Ustiug to Kursk and Chuguev. And in 1648 Moscow itself witnessed a mutiny, the results of which permit one to call it a revolution.

This mutiny was started in Moscow by the rabble, who were aided by the *streltsy;* the movement was supported by the gentry and ended with the capitulation of the government. In accord with the desire of the populace, the government undertook a general review of current legislation with the clear purpose of democratizing it - "that justice and punishment be equitable in the Muscovite state in all matters and for people of all classes, from the highest to the lowest rank." This tendency toward democratization was heatedly condemned by the Patriarch Nikon, who was indignant that the new law drawn up in the *Ulozhenie* of 1648-49[2] recognized the same system of justice for him, the Patriarch, as for the *strelets* (the lowest service man) and the *muzhik* (the lowest tax-paying individual). This tendency was also remarked upon by certain Swedes who were spending the fall of 1648 in Moscow. They reported from Moscow to Sweden that "here they are working diligently to assure that the simple people and others are satisfied by good laws and freedom."

In speaking of democratization, however, we should remember that this term had a conditional sense in Russia at that time. Those who benefited from the movement of 1648 were not the lower social classes in our sense of the word, not the peasantry on the lands of landlords or the bondmen in private households - not, in a word, the enserfed masses on whose labor the private sector of the economy was based. These not only remained in their former condition of enslavement but were subjected to still stricter supervision and more exact registration. Those who benefited from the national disturbances were the middle layers of society, which were placed between the highest level of society, the boiars and the higher clergy, and the enserfed masses. These middle layers were made up of landed gentry, merchants and *posadskie liudi*. The cooperation of these elements of society in 1612 had ended the Time of Troubles; now in 1648 it intimidated the government. The political victory of these social groups was reflected in the *Ulozhenie* of 1648-49 by a whole series of statutes that created a new organization of towns, strengthened the right of landowners over peasant labor, abolished the legal privileges of the clergy and thereby established the principle of the equality of rights of the middle and aristocratic upper classes of Russian society.

This was a portentous moment in the internal history of Russia. During the troubled days of the Russian mutiny of 1648 and in the weeks following, the political consciousness of the bulk of the gentry was significantly sharpened. The gentry, which upon various pretexts had gathered at that time in Moscow in large numbers, departed from its customary obedience to the authorities and addressed the government not in its former tone of petition but in another language, delivering its desires in the form of an ultimatum. This first happened on June 10, 1648, and from that date oppositionist speeches were heard and ultimatums were sounded more than once among the gentry. The gentry became conscious of its class unity and sensed its proportionate weight. The same thing was equally apparent among the commercial and business groups of the populace. These groups forcefully advanced their aims and staunchly defended their interests. The struggle for their city markets and for business with elements of society outside their town, the desire to subordinate to their town all its tax-paying populace so that no one could escape taxation, the desire to banish foreigners from internal Russian markets - all this was pursued with extraordinary energy and persistence by the traders and *posadskie liudi*. In the end they won their victory, and in so doing exhibited all the features of conscious class effort. From this time one can speak of public life in the Muscovite state.

From the time of the revolutionary shocks of 1648 the government ceased to direct completely the life of the society subordinate to it and to pursue only its own interests. It even began to fear its own subjects and, during its first fits of fear of revolution, sought to mobilize foreigners for its defense. As a result of the events of 1648 Tsar Alexis considered the formation of a strong detachment of "household troops" for the personal defense of the Tsar and his family, under the supreme command of his father-in-law, Ivan D. Miloslavsky, who "relied very much on the Dutch," and under the supervision of the Dutch colonel, Buchofen. Rumors of this were rife in Moscow throughout 1648-49. In the end, Buchofen's detachment was formed not of foreigners, but of "gentry cavalrymen," and soon displayed lack of discipline, not wishing to obey foreign officers.[3] The unreliability of this gentry guard led Tsar Alexis to form dependable units of "palace *streltsy*" and "palace infantry," whose personnel were specially selected and who also guarded the Russian palace and enjoyed the Tsar's special favors.

II   The Sudden Change in the Social Life of Russia and the Beginning of the Emancipation of the Personality. New Men (F. M. Rtishchev and A. L. Ordin-Nashchokin. A. S. Matveev and Prince V. V. Golitsyn. G. K. Kotoshikhin)

Close acquaintance with the course of Russian life during the period we have described allows one to imagine all the power and depth of the spiritual shocks through which Russian society had passed. According to a contemporary expression, "the whole world was reeling." Let us remember that after the revolutionary outbursts and the acute class conflict of the first years of Tsar Alexis' reign, there followed ecclesiastical discord, the deposition of Nikon and the schism he provoked. Then the mutiny of Razin erupted. Public life became so stormy that only minds that were too sluggish could remain in peaceful equanimity. Life became a long series of theoretical questions and practical problems in the most diverse spheres of governmental and private activity. To answer these questions and resolve these problems it was necessary to turn to the most diverse authorities and seek the most diverse means.

The time had passed, and not yet long ago, when it had seemed possible to inspire faith in the resurrection of the dead and the immortality of the soul by governmental measures, as had been done with Prince Khvorostinin, or to sentence someone to death for the slightest independence of opinion, as had happened to Prince Shakhovskoi. In this new situation Tsar Alexis himself considered it necessary to support the freedom of religious feeling on the part of secular people who did not wish to fast and pray by arrangement. He agreed with them that ecclesiastical authority "can compel no one to believe in God by force." The old exclusiveness was forgotten and the old authorities faded away. Without hesitation the government turned abroad for guidance: to the Greek East in ecclesiastical affairs, to the West for technical remedies.

Private individuals defined their "orientation" with great freedom and according to the bent of their mind and taste. The observer is amazed by the diversity of cultural types who suddenly spring into view from the depths of a Russian society that not long ago had been wrapped in slumber. When one has become acquainted with some of them, he perceives that their common feature was exactly that freedom of self-development that had been lacking in their fathers' generation. Their fathers had feared to express themselves even in their intimate letters and autobiographical notes. Prince Semen Shakhovskoi, for example, after he had "committed mortal offences," wrote his own biography with such caution that nothing can be learned from it except his "services" and his exiles. He tells of himself only those things that he really cannot conceal. The next generation not only spoke and wrote more freely but acted more freely. Later we shall see how openly and sharply Ordin-Nashchokin expounded his views to Tsar Alexis. We shall see how other figures freely revealed their attitudes and thoughts. What happened can be termed the emancipation of the individual in Russian life. Of course, this was merely the first degree of emancipation, not the unconditional freedom of conscience and thought, but only what we have already termed the freedom of self-development. To understand this we shall cite several concrete examples and shall examine several figures who are characteristic of the times.

Let us dwell in the first instance upon the friends of Tsar Alexis: Rtishchev and Ordin - Nashchokin. After what has already been written concerning them,[4] there is no need to relate their biographies in detail. For our purpose it is enough to recall the typical traits of their intellectual outlook. Better than all others, they serve as symbols of their times.

Feodor Mikhailovich Rtishchev was almost the same age as Tsar Alexis and was numbered among his "chamber" (that is, his closest) courtiers. His court duties caused him to be inseparable from the sovereign, accompanying him even on campaigns. For this reason he possessed great authority and influence in Muscovite ruling circles. But he did not attempt to use this influence for his personal advancement or profit. He had other interests. Rtishchev surrendered himself completely to his soul's attraction to goodness and served it as he understood it. To him goodness was the worship of God in the spirit and in truth, according to the words of the Gospels, and he sought truth in Christian learning, by helping in every way to strengthen theological scholarship in Moscow and settling learned theologians in the city.

Without denying the forms of old Muscovite ritualism, Rtishchev warmly sympathized with the idea of church renewal through activity such as that of Vonifatiev's private circle, as well as of Nikon's official reform. He was the friend and admirer of the educated Ukrainians who came to Moscow on the summons and personal initiative of the Tsar and endeavored in every way to improve their lot and their living conditions. To him is attributed the founding of an entire community of learned Ukrainian monks in the "foreign" St. Andrew's Monastery near Moscow. All leading ecclesiastical circles in the Muscovite state and in the Ukraine - Great Russians, Ukrainians and Greeks alike - loved Rtishchev and respected him as a zealot of enlightenment and a friend and patron of scholars.

If Rtishchev's mind fed upon discussions "with those who were wise and refined by divine scripture," his heart was always moved to charity for the poor and the sick, in which Rtishchev also saw "the spirit and truth" of faith. His contemporaries, who conferred upon Rtishchev the nickname of "the merciful man," spoke with amazement and admiration of his unusual kindness and his acts of brotherly love. Never one to boast of his good deeds (which at times cost him his peace and health), Rtishchev was quick to help not only his countrymen but even foreigners, collecting on the field of battle even the enemy's wounded and caring for them along with Russian soldiers.

Rtishchev's educational and charitable activities are distinguished by one interesting characteristic: they were not limited to the narrow realm of personal life and private dealings but always strove to become social work. When he sought instruction from the Kievan scholars who had been summoned to Moscow, Rtishchev did not simply maintain an acquaintance with them but organized them into a teaching brotherhood in the "foreign" St. Andrew's Monastery, then turned that brotherhood into a center of instruction for society. Rtishchev did not limit his charity to gifts to private individuals, but established hospitals, almshouses and houses of charity, where he gave the sick and the weak temporary or continuous refuge. Upon this work he spent his own personal resources and funds entrusted to him by the Tsaritsa Maria Il'inichna. One of Rtishchev's institutions of this sort outlived him and existed at the time of Peter the Great under the name, "the Hospital of Feodor Rtishchev."

The philanthropy of "the merciful man" served as a model for similar undertakings by the government. It brought the concept of organized charity to the attention of Russians, and from the 1680's this concept was adopted by the Muscovite government.

By such means, which were original for his times, Rtishchev participated in directing the social life of Moscow. And this explains the secret of Rtishchev's broad popularity and the moral influence that he had upon his contemporaries.

Although Rtishchev was not in the first ranks of the Muscovite administration, everyone knew him and turned to him for the most diverse reasons. They allowed him to take the initiative in enacting the most important legislation of the day and gathered in his home to discuss the burning questions of the moment. Rtishchev was at the same time as near and dear to those who adhered to Muscovite antiquity as he was to the innovators. The Patriarch Nikon intimately conversed with Rtishchev and considered him a friend. But in his home the famous Avvakum [5] "made much noise" with Nikon's followers about faith and the law. Rtishchev was one of Avvakum's most agreeable benefactors ("our old comrade, Feodor Rtishchev," as Avvakum called him). Ukrainians and Greeks who arrived in Moscow turned to Rtishchev as to a friend and intercessor. The well known Krizhanich [6] resorted to him with an exposition of his views and theories. In short, Rtishchev's personality attracted people of absolutely all tendencies.

Rtishchev's eminence and influence were to some extent responsible for this. But people were in the main attracted by his perpetual goodness, the breadth of his comprehension and the objectivity that was a fruit of his spiritual originality. In his unusual personality, which was alien to factions and strife and confident of the religious foundation of man's work and thought, humble yet independent of and alien to importunity, his contemporaries first of all saw the nobility of a free spirit and the beauty of one who was conscious of goodness. Not without reason was his biography composed soon after his death. Set in the form of the "lives of the saints," it bestowed the halo of sanctity upon "the merciful man, Feodor Rtishchev."

Thus Rtishchev's qualities and services were honored like those of Archimandrite Dionisius, whose "life," as we know, also appeared immediately after his death. In reality, both these figures of the seventeenth century resembled each other in their extraordinary moral force. But the brilliant monk was active in the twilight before the dawn of cultural life in Russia, while the humane magnate lived in the full dawning of that life. For this reason Rtishchev, and not Dionisius, was better known by his contemporaries and by later generations as well.

Rtishchev's contemporary, Afanasy Lavrentievich Ordin-Nashchokin, was a man of quite another mold. The two had in common only their inner probity. In all else they can be contrasted with each other. Rtishchev regarded involvement in practical government work a digression, as it were, from his usual life in court circles and in the company of his learned friends. Ordin-Nashchokin, on the other hand, spent himself completely in administration and diplomacy, leaving himself no time for philosophizing or even simple rest. He passed his entire life in the uninterrupted turmoil of administrative work, at times conferring with the *Posol'skii prikaz,* or serving in embassies, or away on campaign. And when excessive toil broke his health and finally marred his character, he went to rest in a monastery in the God-forsaken place from which he had come.

Afanasy Lavrentievich had come from the service gentry of Pskov. Around Pskov, in the "inlets" of the city, many families of the Ordin-Nashchokins had settled since the sixteenth century. Although they traced their line back to the clan of a boiar from Pskov,

Nashchoka, who had moved from Tver to Moscow in the days of Simeon the Proud, they had "grown poor." They had not retained their boiar status and sank to the depths of the Russian provincial nobility, settling on *pomestie* estates around Pskov, Opochka and Ostrov. Afanasy Lavrentievich's grandfather, Denis (his nickname was the Warrior) Gavrilovich, had owned a substantial number of villages and much wasteland and under Ivan the Terrible had led his fellow "landlords *[pomeshchiki]* of Pskov" on campaigns against Lithuania. Afanasy's father, however, was not distinguished for anything, and Afanasy himself began his service most ordinarily, among the common nobility.

He is mentioned for the first time in documents of the seventeenth century that are already known to us, in the retinue of an embassy that was sent to adjust the border with Sweden in 1642. It seems that Nashchokin's appointment to the staff of the commission of border demarcation came about because he was considered very familiar with life in the western borderlands of the Muscovite state. It was said of him that "he knows German affairs well and knows German customs as well." There are hints that, because he came from the border regions of Pskov, Afanasy Lavrentievich became familiar with the German language while still a youth, understood Latin and generally experienced the influence of the neighboring German culture. This, of course, determined the course of his service career. He was continually engaged in duties that were connected in one way or another with the western outlying regions. But when his diplomatic skills were revealed during negotiations with Sweden, the government made him a professional diplomat.

After he gained the affection and personal friendship of Tsar Alexis, Nashchokin became a member of the *boiar duma,* attained boiar status and was the first to be given the title of chancellor, which was translated in Moscow by the very complicated formula, "Guardian of the Great Royal Seals and the Great Ambassadorial Affairs." By this time he had become the director of the *Posol'skii prikaz,* which theretofore had included the ambassadorial *diaki* who were subordinate to the *boiar duma.* His personal direction introduced something new to this department. Until then the *Posol'skii prikaz* had been subordinated to an executive board under the *boiar duma*. Henceforth it became something of an organ for the personal policy of its director, insofar as this policy was approved by the sovereign. Earlier it had been impossible to speak of the personal political views of this or that person in the government. All the boiars had simply "had a talk," until they all agreed "on one statement," then they "passed their decision," and their "decision" was executed by the *Posol'skii prikaz* with the ratification of the sovereign. But under this new regime the views and actions of the director of the department were moulded by his personal policies, which were implemented with the consent and approval of Tsar Alexis, while the *boiar duma* retained sanctions and purely formal representation in this area. It is precisely this new order that affords us an opportunity to study Nashchokin's political orientation and to characterize him as a statesman.

Throughout his entire life this native of the territory of Pskov retained the local impressions and notions acquired during his youth. For him the interests of the western borderlands of Russia always came first.[7] His constant dream was to strengthen Russian influence on the Baltic coast and to obtain for Russia an outlet to the Baltic Sea. Like someone from Pskov, his typical inclination was toward the Gulf of Riga and the Western Dvina, and not toward the Gulf of Finland and the Neva. The object of his yearnings was not Narva, but Riga.

As a director of Russian foreign policy, he faced the choice of pursuing one of two immediate tasks: either to struggle with the Polish Commonwealth for the Little Russian Ukraine or to obtain the Baltic seacoast from Sweden. He was entirely in favor of the latter and adhered to the idea that Little Russia was not worth the sacrifices its acquisition would entail, and that it would be better to ally with the Poles than to remain hostile to them. He even expressed the hope that if such a union were achieved, it would occasion the unification of all the South Slavic peoples around Russia and Poland. From this point of view, strife between Russia and Poland over the Ukraine seemed to him a baneful civil war. It would also preclude harmonious operations by Russia and Poland against the Swedes, whose hegemony on the Baltic was equally unacceptable to both. As long as Ordin-Nashchokin was able to secure Tsar Alexis' agreement, he implemented his system to the

Second Half of the Seventeenth Century

extent, of course, that it did not interfere with the current course of events. But when Tsar Alexis succumbed to other influences and, despite his chancellor, came to the final conclusion that the question of Little Russia and the struggle with Poland was paramount at that moment, Ordin-Nashchokin was dismissed. The advance toward the Baltic was thus postponed to the time of Peter the Great, but its necessity had been correctly predicted by Nashchokin.

Nashchokin was conscious of more than the commercial importance of the western routes. He understood that through these routes European culture, of which he was an advocate, could enter Russia more easily. As a native of Pskov, he had experienced it in his everyday life and accepted it as something usual and unavoidable for ordinary Russian life. His acute intellect assimilated the principles of the European political system and economic order of his day. He appeared as the earliest spokesman in Moscow for the concepts of bureaucratic absolutism and mercantilism. When he met foreign diplomats on ambassadorial business, he stood on the same cultural level with them and impressed them as a European in Russian dress. Although he maintained the external forms of Russian society, he was in essence already a reformed man. As V. O. Kliuchevsky has said, "Ordin-Nashchokin in many ways anticipated and first expressed many of the ideas that the Reformer (Peter the Great) translated into reality." In the realm of practical policy he was thus a figure with an entirely new mentality, and one who was estranged from the ancient Muscovite traditions.

He was alien to these traditions in his moral bent as well. He was sickened by the old Muscovite custom of conducting affairs in keeping with considerations of seniority and personal profit, of catering to "pedigree" at the expense of personal ability, and of favoring personal profit over the common good. With bitterness he wrote to the Tsar from one of his embassies: "In Moscow, Sovereign, even government affairs are treated slackly and negligently . . . . Ambassadorial *diaki* who participate in negotiations at conferences have not yet learned to give the affairs of state the highest respect they deserve, while those living in Moscow fearlessly confuse foreign affairs with problems of personal income from bribes and managing public houses." When he quarreled with the proud and aristocratic boiars, Nashchokin explained to the Tsar that he acted not out of personal hostility, but because his "heart ached for the affairs of state, and I cannot remain silent when I see someone's negligence in affairs of state." He observed that "we favor a cause or oppose it not because of the cause itself, but because of the man who supports it. I am not liked, and therefore my cause is scorned."[8]

Nashchokin himself served his cause selflessly and protected his reputation in the service with great scrupulousness. In the heat of the conflicts that arose, he more than once asked the Tsar "to relieve him, lest the affairs of state be damaged," for he considered it possible to work only with the Tsar's complete trust.

He came to complete despair when his own son, Voin, remained abroad as a traitor while participating in an official mission, taking with him official funds and "many state documents and records." When the stricken father requested that he himself be dismissed, the Tsar responded by sending him, "from us, your Great Sovereign, a word of kindness." This word was not only kind, but touching. After many laudatory epithets to Afanasy Lavrentievich, "you, one who loves Christ, peace, the poor and hard work," the Tsar warmly expressed his own sympathy not only for Nashchokin himself but also to Nashchokin's wife and stressed that he sympathized with them in "their great sorrow and tribulations." He would not even hear of dismissing his "fervent minister and supporter," for he did not consider the father guilty of his son's treason. The Tsar himself had trusted the son as much as he had the father. "And now, faithful servant of Christ and your Sovereign, stop explaining the foolishness of your son and your trust in him. Your Great Sovereign himself received your son in secret more than once and entrusted him with much information intended for you, never suspecting that there was such dangerous poison under his tongue."

The Tsar also attempted to console the father with the hope that the youth would return, and that he was perhaps not a traitor but had merely been foolish. "We, the Great Sovereign, are therefore not amazed that your son should go astray. We know that he did so because of his lack of strength. He is a young man who wishes to see all of

God's creation and His creatures in this world. He is like a bird that flies here and there, but when he has flown enough, returns to the nest. So, too, your son will remember his temporal nest and also that spiritual home provided him by the Holy Spirit at baptism and will come back to you soon."

This letter from Tsar Alexis, which is especially touching, sufficed to keep Nashchokin at his work in this instance. When the fugitive, Voin, repented and returned from his flight, the father did not intercede with the Tsar on his behalf, and the gentleness of the punishment that was imposed on the son did not result from petitions by Nashchokin.

Rtishchev and Ordin-Nashchokin are two striking examples of the "new men" of the seventeenth century. In departing from the centuries-old Muscovite routine, they liberated their personalities from it, yet they did not submit to another way of life. Perhaps it is because of this that they remained such distinctive personalities.

The pair of progressive Russian dignitaries who followed them and occupied Nashchokin's position - the chancellors A. S. Matveev and V. V. Golitsyn - are more definite in their orientation than in their characters. Both followed the path of imitation and borrowings and began to live in "the Polish manner" or "the German manner." Capable and intelligent men, they sensibly executed their official duties and probably enjoyed favor at court for good reason, because their qualities set them apart from the surrounding court and administrative milieu. Prince V. V. Golitsyn loved to introduce into everyday practice humane ideas and grand designs not very well elaborated or defined. Matveev, however, did not have this weakness and remained only a practical bureaucrat, not rising to abstract principles and lofty feelings in his practical relationships. Neither was malicious by nature or governed sternly, Golitsyn in particular. With his name are associated several humane measures that imparted to the entire regime of his day (1683-89) an especially gentle cast. All these traits characterize these men to some extent, but it is difficult to go beyond such traits in determining their individuality. Their most striking quality still remains their inclination to imitate the West.

As far as Matveev is concerned, his attitude toward the question of borrowing "overseas" things and customs for use in Russia was, so to speak, mundane. He liked one or another aspect of the foreign life that he knew and readily transferred it to his own home, adopted it to his way of life or even recommended it to the Tsar. In so doing he raised no questions of principle and made no generalizations. Apparently he did not have to defend his views and conduct, because at that time the defensive tendency in Moscow was already very weak and no one threatened punishment for intimacy with foreigners. Artamon Sergeevich was even married to a Russified Scottish woman, Evdokiia Grigorievna Hamilton, for which no one reproached him. During the reign of Tsar Alexis, Matveev suffered not for his closeness to foreigners and his outlook, but because of court intrigue.

Until his misfortune and exile Matveev lived merrily and freely. He maintained his home "in the European manner," furnished it with foreign furniture and trinkets and established for himself a theatrical company under the director Johann Gottfried and the scene-painter Peter Ingles ("a master in painting in perspective"). Hired foreigners and house serfs of the Matveevs performed in this company. Matveev's home theatre along with his orchestra was presented to the court, and the Tsar and the Tsaritsa (who was Matveev's pupil) amused themselves with "comedies" on Biblical themes, including the comedy, "How the Queen Cut Off the Head of King Holofernes." To ensure that the company continued successfully, it was ordered that clerks be sent to the director, Gottfried, "to learn the business of comedy," while urchins were recruited from the Novomeshchansky settlement "as comedians." S. M. Soloviev has remarked, not without humor, that "thus a theatrical school was founded in Moscow before the Slavic-Latin-Greek Academy!"

Tsar Alexis, who was inclined to amusement of any sort, encouraged his favorite, Matveev, to borrow in the field of entertainment. Both of them had a great weakness for foreign things of this sort. The Tsar, for example, noted with his own hand in official papers that he wished to receive from abroad "a carriage, like the one in which the kings of Spain and France and Caesar go about, experts who make birds sing in the trees, people who play trumpets and experts in making comedy." Because the Tsar expressed this desire to have "experts in making comedy" ten years before Matveev's company appeared (in 1660), we can assume that the Tsar's favorite established his company simply to fulfill the wishes of his sovereign.

A man of greater principle than Matveev was Prince Vasily Vasilievich Golitsyn. We have little data to use in determining his personal characteristics. But everything that we have speaks of his kindness and humanity. On the one hand, the legislation of the years when Golitsyn was in power is notable for its gentleness. On the other, the foreigner, Neuville, to whom we are indebted for the sole characterization of Golitsyn, pictures him as a political dreamer, filled with good intentions of every sort. Unfortunately, Neuville was unable to transmit in detail all that Golitsyn said to him, and Professor V. O. Kliuchevsky's attempt to develop Neuville's allusions goes no further than hypotheses, shrewd but not always indisputable.[9]

If we agree with Kliuchevsky that Golitsyn's dreams formed a whole system of reforms, then we must understand that this enlightened dignitary intended first of all to free the peasants from the rule of the landowners and from military obligation, in their stead raising the taxes imposed on the peasantry. The treasury would use this increased revenue for the maintenance of the armed forces, which would consist strictly of nobles. To provide this service, the nobility would have to be prepared for it abroad, then would comprise the great bulk of the regular army. Their sojourn abroad would not only provide technical training but would raise the general cultural level of this class.

Thus motives of a military-technical, social-economic and educational nature were intertwined in Golitsyn's plans. Neuville, who was fascinated by Golitsyn, concludes his panegyric to him by saying: "If I should wish to write all that I learned from this prince, I would never finish. Suffice it to say that he wished to populate the deserts, enrich the poor, turn savages into human beings, cowards into brave men and the huts of herdsmen into stone palaces."

So radical in his general plans for reform, Golitsyn in his private life also departed sharply from traditional Muscovite ways in favor of those of the cultured West. Here is how V. O. Kliuchevsky, using documents that have been preserved, described Golitsyn's everyday life:

> In his spacious home in Moscow, which foreigners considered one

of the most magnificent in all Europe, everything was arranged in the European manner. In the large halls the wall space between windows was filled with large mirrors. The walls were hung with pictures, portraits of Russian and foreign sovereigns and German geographical maps in golden frames. On the ceilings the planetary system was painted. Many clocks and thermometers of artistic workmanship decorated the rooms. Golitsyn had a large library of various manuscripts and printed books in Russian, Polish and German . . . . Golitsyn's home was a meeting place for educated foreigners who came to Moscow, and his hospitality toward them surpassed that of other Muscovites who favored foreigners, for he even received Jesuits, which the others could not condone.

Golitsyn's career was interrupted by the political coup of 1689, when the "lady ruler," Sophia Alexeevna, was removed from power. Golitsyn was also removed with her, and his splendid home was confiscated and liquidated. One concise inventory of this home comprised an entire book, which was full of valuable indications of the kind of external cultural surroundings in which the "great" Golitsyn had lived.

If we descend from the heights of Russian society to its middle layers, we shall also find a representative of this same movement toward innovation. It is sufficient to point out the well-known Kotoshikhin to become convinced of the degree of radicalism that had become accessible to the ordinary Muscovite of that epoch.

A simple clerk in the *Posol'skii prikaz,* Grigory Karpovich Kotoshikhin was, according to his contemporaries, "distinguished in intellect above his generation and countrymen." Because he was an intelligent and capable man, he was sent as a "herald" to Reval and Stockholm to carry on diplomatic relations with the Swedes. But his familiarity with the Swedes was not limited to his official trips. Kotoshikhin also maintained friendships with Swedish agents who lived permanently in Moscow. In the end this Russian clerk became "a good Swede." He began to spy in the *Posol'skii prikaz* for money given him by the Swedes, turned documents over to them, communicated to them information that they needed, and then (in 1664) quit the Muscovite state completely and went to Sweden, traveling through Lübeck and Narva.

In Sweden he changed his last name from Kotoshikhin to Selitsky and exchanged Orthodoxy for Protestantism. He was received into the Swedish service and composed for the Swedish government a detailed description of the Muscovite state, in which he expresses his Protestant viewpoint. In speaking of how "icons that had been painted in ancient times" were sent ahead of Russian embassies and regiments, he raises the question: "Why do they send these icons?" And he replies: "For this reason, that when in the course of a war a victory is achieved against the enemy, or when an embassy is able to win peace, and these things are realized through the grace of God, they believe that it was done through the help and intercession and prayers of the Mother of God or the saints whose likenesses are on the icons. And because of such reasoning they are not ashamed to talk to these lifeless objects and ask them for help, so blind are they. The devil has blinded them with his unquenchable fire."[10]

A more striking proof of Kotoshikhin's religious apostasy is difficult to imagine. In the light of these quoted sentences we can well understand his other railings against the Russian people, such as when he said: "In their state they teach nothing good and accept only arrogance, shamelessness, hatred and untruth." In short, Kotoshikhin completely separated himself from his native soil and adopted another "faith, custom and happy liberty."

III The Situation of Foreigners in Russia in the Second Half of the Century. Russified Commercial Families and Foreign Officers and Doctors

These characteristics of the "new" Russian men that we have adduced in cursory fashion suffice, we think, to confirm the justice of our remarks concerning the freedom of individual self-development that was attained in the seventeenth century. The sudden change of public attitudes after the revolutionary outbursts of the middle of the century opened a broad path for every sort of innovation and in the end shattered the foundations of the old way of life. Adherents of olden times, such as the famous Archpriest Avvakum and the equally stubborn Deacon Feodor, who so resembles him, had to struggle not only against ecclesiastical reform, but also against "the spirit of the times" in general. They had to defend not only the old ritual and texts, but all of the "old Rus" that was clearly passing away under the pressure of "novelties."

Despite Kotoshikhin's sceptical assertion, progressive Russians willingly "accepted good learning," that is, improved their culture by borrowing from abroad. By the end of the seventeenth century the foreign element in Moscow had blossomed into a splendid flower. What in the first half of the century had been a timorous experiment had now become a habitual practice. Conditions of life had greatly changed. So much that was new made its appearance that we would need an entire book to enumerate each kind of borrowing that became part of the Russian way of life. We can give merely the most general listing of what can be regarded as characteristic phenomena within the limits of our study.

To begin with, masses of foreigners were now engaged in the commercial life of Russia and in service to the state. A Jesuit who arrived in Moscow at the end of the seventeenth century discovered, to his great astonishment, that in the German suburb near Moscow "there were almost all European nationalities." In his opinion, Catholics were outnumbered by the "heretical" Protestants, but there were still a great many of them. Even the idea of a Jesuit living in Moscow is indicative, for their entry into the Muscovite state hitherto had been strictly forbidden.

The majority of the foreigners in Russia were Dutch and English. As far as the English were concerned, the restrictive measures that had been enacted against them in 1649 were still in force, but were not strictly applied, for the Muscovite government, as before, found direct advantage for itself in maintaining commercial relations with the English market. After Moscow had replied to the execution of King Charles I with repression, it did not think to maintain this repression

Second Half of the Seventeenth Century

and did not close the roads to Russia to English goods and English emigrants. Therefore the English merchant and the English (or Scottish) officer was not a rarity in Russian life during the second half of the seventeenth century. They only yielded first place to the Dutch as the most favored nation.

At the end of the century there were more than 300 Dutch merchants in the Muscovite state. The entire foreign commercial colony in Moscow comprised more than 1,000 persons. The Dutch merchants seem to have been organized. They comprised a "hundred" under the supremacy of a "chief," and the Muscovite administration officially recognized this hundred "of the foreign traders of the Dutch lands and the city of Hamburg."

Many of these service and commercial foreigners became firmly attached to Russian soil. In whole families and even in groups of related families they made themselves at home in Moscow, converted to Orthodoxy, were favored with official acts of kindness and, even more importantly, won the trust of the authorities and became their agents in commercial and diplomatic affairs. Some families developed their commercial and business operations to such an extent and became so close to the administration that they gained a certain influence and enjoyed public fame. The new *gostinyi dvor* in Kitaigorod was their formal center, and there they had their storehouses. "In this court," says one contemporary, Kilburger, "the foreigners kept what we might call their exchange and their assembly, and there they could meet every day." At the upper level of this class of capitalists were ten or so names of those who were especially privileged and important. Of these we can name, for example, the van Klenks, the Marselis family and the Vinius family. Each of these families is typical in its own way.

The family of van Klenks had traded in Russia for many decades, and their representatives had lived in Moscow for a long time. They had been granted charters for privileged trade by Tsars Michael and Alexis and had been honored with the title of *"gosti."* One of the van Klenks had even gone to Moscow as the Dutch ambassador in 1675 and had been very well received in this capacity. But the van Klenks did not abandon their native land for Russia. After extensive operations in Moscow they still returned to their own homeland. To them Muscovy remained merely a market, which they had to use in the interests of Dutch trade and politics. And this the van Klenks did with great skill.

The Marselis family was closer to Russia. Along with their close relatives, the Bernzli, Kellermann, Fentzel and other families, they formed a large nest of capitalistic entrepreneurs in the Muscovite state. They had appeared in Russia at the beginning of the Romanov dynasty, became well settled and undertook every sort of business. The most distinguished representative of the family, Peter Marselis, was the son of the Danish commissioner at the embassy in Moscow and had been born and reared in Moscow. Like his father, he was also considered a Danish commissioner and occasionally executed diplomatic missions, while at the same time his main occupation was iron works in the regions of Tula and Kaluga and in the Pomorie. Peter Marselis' sons, Peter and Leonty, and his grandson, Christian, continued to develop their father's enterprises and, like him, became government agents. They executed various assignments and for several years (1668-75) maintained the newly organized postal service between Moscow and the western frontiers.

The skill of the Marselis family in combining government service with commercial activities served to enrich them. Their connections with government circles made it easy for them to obtain all sorts of concessions and privileges. The biographer of the Marselis family, in tracing their fortunes on Russian soil, says of them: "They were exploiters who knew how to insinuate themselves into the confidence of the government and gain profitable rights for themselves. But at the same time they were energetic people who were able to organize broadly the enterprises they conceived. Their importance to the history of Russian trade and industry during this period is very great. They represented capital in a Russian society that was still living in the realm of a natural economy. They became rich because of that society."

The Vinius family are worth noting because of their attitude toward Russia. The first of them, Andrei Vinius, came to Russia from Holland in about 1630, engaged in buying grain and was able to win the favor of the Muscovite government by buying state grain reserves "at a high price, without ruse and without excessive profits." In 1631 he had already acquired a charter for the right to free trade and in two years won for himself the exclusive right to tax-free production of iron manufactures in the Tula region. The broad scope of Vinius' enterprises at times created financial difficulties and forced him to seek partners (such as the Marselis family, Thielmann Akkema and others). But Vinius' prosperity generally increased, and he enjoyed great fame in the business world, as well as the favor of the authorities. Foreigners found him more devoted to Russians than to his own countrymen, and this was apparently true. Vinius converted to the Orthodox faith, carried out all sorts of missions for the Muscovite government at home and, while abroad, prided himself in his title, which in full was "Andrei Denisov, the Son of Vinius, Commissioner of His Imperial Majesty of the Muscovite State and Muscovite *gost'*."

His son, Andrei Andreevich, was even more distinguished than his father. He won great fame as one of the collaborators of Peter the Great. The government bureaucrat in him was overcome by the merchant and manufacturer. Orthodox by faith, he became Russianized and was soon accepted into service, where he became first "a trader in the *gostinaia sotnia*,"[11] then an interpreter in the *Posol'skii prikaz*, then a Muscovite nobleman and *diak*. As an interpreter he did not merely "translate" during embassies, but engaged in literary translations, authored proposals (concerning the establishment of a fleet) and traveled abroad on diplomatic missions. Subsequently, he went into administration. He directed the *Aptekarskii prikaz* and succeeded Marselis in 1675 as head of the postal service. Until the time of Peter the Great he devoted himself exclusively to Russian administration and became one of Peter's most valuable collaborators, no different from the other "fledgelings in Peter's nest." In 1703 Vinius lost Peter's trust and favors and was about to flee abroad in disgrace in 1706. But he could not bear this "excommunication" and voluntarily returned to Russian service, in which he died in 1717.

Many of the foreigners who served in the Russian armed forces were also Russified. By the end of the seventeenth century the number of soldiers in the regular army was not less than 90,000 men. According to an official count in 1681, there were 29,844 men in the regular cavalry (knights, lancers and dragoons) and 59,203 men in the infantry. A substantial percentage of the commanders of this army were foreigners.

In the opinion of one contemporary (the ambassador of the Holy Roman Empire, Meyerberg, in 1661), there had gathered in Moscow "a countless multitude" of foreign military men. He knew of more than a hundred colonels and generals alone. The exact tally of the foreign officer corps for 1696 sets the number of generals and other officers (including ensigns) at 231 in the cavalry and 723 in the infantry.[12]

Russia's transition from the old forms of military organization to regular European forms was accomplished by an officers corps patterned on the European, in which the guiding role was naturally played by professional military men from the West. At first these were very much indulged in Moscow, for they were badly needed. They were paid a large salary (400 rubles a month for cavalry colonels and 250 rubles for those in the infantry) and were given large *pomestie* estates with Russian peasants. In every possible way they were retained in the service and were hindered from returning abroad. Under these conditions, many foreigners "became veterans" of the Russian service and, once Russified, accepted not only Orthodoxy but even native customs.

"There is a noticeable distinction among officers," one contemporary foreign observer (Schleizing) said of foreigners who served in Moscow.

> Some of them were called old Germans, others new Germans. The old Germans were born in Russia . . . . Their German blood has evaporated. For the most part, they have Russian manners, go about in Russian dress and are very poor at military pursuits, understanding little or nothing of these matters. These miserable fledgelings are like dust in the eyes of the better officers, who find them obnoxious. They can never return to their homeland, for their fathers and grandfathers have taken out eternal citizenship in the (Muscovite) state, and many of them have accepted the Russian faith. The new Germans are those who have been recruited abroad by the Tsar and who earlier served the kings of Sweden, Poland and other lands. There are brave people among them.

As time passed and the influx of foreign military men became so great that the labor and learning that they supplied exceeded Moscow's demand, their situation began to deteriorate somewhat. It began to seem awkward to give *pomestie* estates with peasants to foreigners, even to those who "had been baptized into the Orthodox Christian faith for the sake of piety and the good of the state." Their rate of pay, with which the foreigners alone had been pleased, decreased bit by bit, as did pensions to the widows and children "of the commanders who perished in war or died serving the state." And in 1682 some 383 commanders of other faiths were simply told that "henceforth they would be given no state salary without rendering service. If any wish to remain in Moscow, let them live in their own residences without salary. When they begin to teach military subjects again, the government will pay them again. And if any wish to go somewhere else, the sovereign has ordered that they be dismissed without detention." Thus by the end of the century Moscow began to fill its officer corps exclusively with Russified foreigners and to receive new officers into state service only through special selection.

Under these new conditions for service in Russia, which demanded that a man firmly commit himself, there were still such eminent men as Patrick Gordon and Paul Menezius (or Menezes), both of whom were Catholic, yet who were persons trusted by the Muscovite authorities. Gordon had spent his entire youth in military surroundings. He left his native Scotland early and served the Swedes and the Poles, participating in many campaigns. His bravery, good management and honesty had won him a fine reputation. In 1661, when he was 36 years of age, he simultaneously received two offers of service, in Austria and in Russia. He chose the latter and went to Moscow for a term of three years. But these three years became decades. Gordon lived in Moscow the remaining 38 years of his life, rising to the high rank of general. He won such confidence from the government that he was given an independent diplomatic mission to England.

From Gordon's detailed diary we can see how well foreigners became adjusted to Russian surroundings and what freedom they enjoyed, so long as they did not try to forsake the service of Russia. All of Gordon's attempts to resign and return to his homeland were refused angrily and even with threats to send him and his family into exile. Yet at the same time the highest personages in the government made him their intimate adviser. The distinguished Prince V. V. Golitsyn often summoned Gordon for political discussions that at times were secret in nature. At the beginning of 1684 he asked Gordon to compose for him a detailed memorandum on the question of war with the Crimea, and the next day Gordon presented to him his memoir, which was written without interference from the censor and with great freedom of thought and expression. Gordon's biographer, Professor Alexander Brückner, speaks of this memoir very approvingly, saying that its thoroughness and breadth "can serve as proof that Gordon could expound complicated political problems very clearly and distinctly in the shortest time."[13]

Gordon's great efficiency, his integrity and honesty, his steadfastness and stability of character ensured that his position was not affected by changes of authorities and influence in Moscow. Close to Golitsyn, the Tsarevna Sophia's favorite, Gordon became just as close to Tsar Peter when Peter deposed Sophia and began to rule himself. During the last years of his life Gordon was part of the highest circle of Muscovite officials and, as is known, was one of the most honored of Peter's favorites.

Paul Menezius, "Baron von Pitfodels," was not as successful in his career. He was unable to become as eminent an adviser as Gordon. But he was no less trusted by the Muscovite government. Despite the fact that he was a good Catholic *("huomo dotto e bonissimo cattolico,"* as was attested in Rome), he enjoyed a fine reputation in Russia and more than once executed diplomatic missions, representing Moscow even in Rome. His education and adroitness made a great impression at the Papal Court. He was considered a wholly educated man, and it was remarked that he had mastered the French, English (he was a Scot by birth), German and Latin languages. He supposedly spoke Latin with special fluency and refinement.

His position in Moscow was secure not only because of the merits of his work but because through his Scottish relatives, the Hamiltons, he was related by marriage to the Matveevs and the Naryshkins. His closeness to these two families, which were related, served Menezius as a firm foundation. It was precisely because of this closeness that the famous legend was created that Tsar Alexis Mikhailovich had appointed

Second Half of the Seventeenth Century

Menezius the tutor of his son, Peter *("le déclara gouverneur de jeune prince Pierre son fils, auprés duquel il a toujours demeuré jusqu'au commencement du règne du czar Jean").* Even if there is not a grain of truth in this story, it is interesting that a foreign favorite in the Russian palace is first presented to us in this light.

In concluding our remarks about the foreigners who were active in Russia during the second half of the seventeenth century, we must mention the status of medical affairs at that time. Gone now was the old Muscovite practice of considering an arriving foreign doctor and his medicaments the exclusive property of the Tsar, to be used only by him and to be controlled by the boiars closest to the Tsar. To obtain medicine from this supply of drugs in the days of Tsar Michael, a special petition had been required, as well as "the Sovereign's own decree."[14] Later a "new apothecary" was opened in Moscow, from which medicines were sold freely "to people of all ranks." The income from this apothecary supported the *Aptekarskii prikaz* or *Aptekarskaia palata.*

In the second half of the seventeenth century medicine emerged from its former office in the palace into the realm of government. It was constituted a special department and apparently began to develop quite rapidly. The *Aptekarskii prikaz* dealt with the invitation of physicians from abroad and with the training of Russian surgeons. It oversaw their service; it was their court of appeal; it established apothecaries, gardens and fields of medicinal herbs and sent physicians and medical remedies to the troops in the field.

Under the jurisdiction of this department medical personnel rapidly increased in number. During the days of Tsar Michael, Russia had not had more than twenty doctors (those who treated internal diseases) and surgeons (those who treated external diseases).[15] But during the reign of Tsar Alexis not less than thirteen new doctors, twenty-seven surgeons and an oculist were invited from abroad. When Peter the Great came to the throne in 1682 Moscow had six doctors, nineteen surgeons and thirty-six lesser medical personnel ("surgical students"), not counting doctors and surgeons in other towns and in the armed forces. These figures are not negligible. The Russian people were correct when they said that they had in their midst "many surgeons from all lands, who live in Moscow." They were also correct in saying that "the sovereign has foreign doctors from many lands, as well as some native to the Muscovite state."

We have sufficient evidence that the Russian people began to adopt the medical science of these foreigners. During the Azov campaign of 1695 seven Russian surgeons were added to the fourteen foreign surgeons in the army. In Moscow itself there were dozens of them. In 1682 there were forty-four Russian surgeons and surgical students under the jurisdiction of the *Aptekarskii prikaz*. The range of their knowledge is defined by the words of one of these Russian specialists: "I heal wounds from shot and cure fractures and stab wounds. I cut out bullets and know how to draw blood from the veins through suction and how to distill vodka. I can also mix salves and know how to treat internal diseases. I also know a bit about treating eyes and bones." In short, we encounter in the same person a surgeon, orthopedist, therapeutist, oculist, pharmacist and, in the expression of the time, a home-brewer *[samogonshchik]*.

The present state of medical knowledge and technique causes us to smile at these Russian experiments in doctoring. But we should mention that for this epoch the partial emancipation of medical practice permitted by the Russian authorities is of great importance. By the end of the seventeenth century the Russian people could be cured not only by native quacks from "the green stalls" (chandlery shops), but by surgeons who had completed the medical schools of the West and who were at least quasi-scientifically prepared for their work.

IV *Ukrainians and Greeks and Their "Teachings." Scholasticism and Polish Influence*

Contemporaneous with the influx of people from Western Europe, a stream of people flowed into Moscow from the Ukraine. We have already pointed out that in the middle of the seventeenth century the Russian authorities began to summon learned Ukrainians into the Muscovite state not only for the work of correcting books of public worship but to renew in general Orthodox theological knowledge in

Moscow. The Polish War (1654-1667) of Tsar Alexis led to the conquest of the Ukraine and, most importantly, of Kiev, the center of Ukrainian learning. The schools and monasteries where the intellectual forces of the region were concentrated were now, after the Muscovite victories, subject to Moscow. Their relations with Moscow were facilitated and simplified.

At the same time Nikon's so-called ecclesiastical reform demanded more and more experienced people, who were simultaneously recruited from the Greek East and the Ukraine. These circumstances brought to Moscow a mass of Little Russians and some White Russians of the most diverse professions and types - from highly educated and literarily gifted intellectuals and courtiers to humble, hard-working folk, who could "raise every kind of animal and bird."

By the end of the seventeenth century so many strangers had appeared in Russian monasteries that, in the words of one researcher, "some Muscovite cloisters were filled with them." Strangers from abroad even gained control of many monasteries, a circumstance that brought reproach from one of the eastern Patriarchs (Dositheos of Jerusalem in 1686). In the presence of Tsars Ivan and Peter Alexeevich he insisted that "in Moscow the old regulations ought to be maintained, and abbots and archimandrites should not be Cossacks, but Muscovites." The Patriarch felt it only normal that "the Muscovite be found both in Moscow and in the Cossack lands, while the Cossack be found only in Cossack lands." But Moscow did not support this petition and allowed Ukrainians to assume governing positions even in the ecclesiastical administration.

Outside the church in palace life, at court and in the economic life of the palace, large numbers of Ukrainians likewise appeared. These were primarily representatives of various applied sciences, arts and trades: icon painters, engravers, distillers and gardeners. A number of these gardeners worked in the royal gardens as vine growers and apiarists. Later, South Russian scholars became teachers in the palace and in the homes of the Muscovite aristocracy. We can cite the names of many of these teachers, who not only taught families but set up small schools in private homes (for example, at the home of F. M. Rtishchev, whom we know). The number of such teachers became so great that it was even proposed that with the establishment of an academy in Moscow, they should be prohibited from giving lessons in private homes, in order not to compete with academic teaching.

Finally, in addition to these teachers and domestic tutors, preachers and orators from Little Russia and White Russia appeared in Moscow. They introduced not only religious sermons but also secular "orations," that is, congratulatory and panegyrical speeches. The custom of delivering speeches on holidays and festivals and of using them to praise heroes and benefactors became established in official Muscovite life. These preachers and orators were heard not only in the churches but at parades and receptions as well, speaking on both ecclesiastical and political themes. At times speeches were commissioned in advance, as a customary and necessary component of some festival or other. Moscow was not satisfied with these southern newcomers and took the trouble to train its own home-grown "orators." The fashion for declamation occasioned, along with "orations," also "verses," which were largely composed for various occasions or were simply borrowed from what was customary in South Russia. They were read or chanted "with secular singing" in the Little Russian manner, that is, with a variety of tunes from the secular popular songs in which the musical Ukrainians could be so brilliant.

By the time of Tsar Feodor (1676-1682) the vogue for everything that was Little Russian, which had embraced the upper levels of Muscovite society, began to dissipate because of Moscow's bitter disappointment in assimilating the Ukraine. The Little Russians proved to be not such loyal citizens as Muscovites had thought when they began their struggle for the Dnieper region. They were "inconstant" and unfaithful. Even in Moscow they frequently appeared to be insincere and self-seeking.

One of the most brilliant representatives of Ukrainian culture in Moscow, Semen Polotsky, notes with bitterness in his correspondence this change in the Muscovite attitude toward Little Russians. He reports that he himself did not suffer from this change, because he "sat peacefully in his cell and did not dash out, like the bee into the frost." But he admits that things were generally worse for Ukrainians in Moscow. He explained that, first of all, in Moscow *"nemo illum amat, qui 'da, da mihi' clamat"* ["No one loves a person who cries, 'Give me, give me.' "], and that "the inconstancy of the Ukraine disgusted us, despite whatever other goodwill it might have had." This he wrote in 1669; and a year later he stated in more detail that because of the behavior of various frivolous persons, Moscow's attitude toward Ukrainians had so changed that some of those who had flown to Moscow, like bees to fragrance, were now ready to change their minds and flee.

We know that the long and very esoteric controversy between Muscovite and Ukrainian theologians concerning transubstantiation had ended unfortunately for the Ukrainians, and the *sobor* of 1690, convened in Moscow by the Patriarch Joachim, condemned the "bread-worshipping" heresy of the Latinized Ukrainians and their Muscovite disciples.[16] Because of this condemnation all Little Russians were brought under the shadow of suspicion that they were generally unorthodox. The position of South Russian scholars in Moscow was so compromised that for some time they were denied access to the upper heirarchy. But Muscovy could not live without them, for it needed their learning and still valued their standard of culture. So throughout the entire second half of the seventeenth century we see in the palace and in the company of the Patriarch influential South Russians, drawn from those whose personal orthodoxy Muscovites could not doubt. The most famous of these were Epiphany Slavinetsky and Semen Polotsky, both of whom were Kievan monks.

Epiphany Slavinetsky lived in Moscow for at least twenty years and died there in 1675. He was a withdrawn scholar who did not strive for worldly successes. On summons from the Muscovite authorities he engaged in correcting books, translated and edited texts of Holy Scripture and the Fathers of the Church, composed sermons, wrote lives of the saints, authored various canonical notes on various problems of ecclesiastical life, and was editor of the *sobor* "acts" (protocols) and definitions of the Muscovite church, as well as of translations of similar texts of the Eastern Church. In his person the Muscovite church acquired an expert who was well versed in all the problems that had arisen at this tumultous and troubled period in the life of church and society. Slavinetsky was, therefore, highly respected and esteemed. But he did not venture out into the arena of public activity, apparently because his nature lacked the essential qualities needed for it.

Semen Polotsky's activity in Moscow, where he appeared in 1663, was of another sort. Lively, convivial, possessed of fine social qualities, he successfully undertook the most diverse activities. At first he taught, and it seems that his pedagogical talents were esteemed in Moscow. From 1667 he became a teacher for the royal family and educated the Tsareviches Alexis and Feodor and the Tsarevna Sophia. He also had pupils among the Russian aristocracy. In addition, Polotsky demonstrated his talent as an author of purely literary works of prose and verse. He composed speeches and salutory addresses, tried his hand at comedy and carried on an extensive correspondence in ornate literary forms with Muscovite and South Russian correspondents.

His pen was called upon for official service as well. He was commissioned to compose official speeches in the name of the Tsar and of church officials for various festive assemblies and meetings. He was charged with editing the *sobor* decisions and "acts." He officially conducted polemics against the schismatic faction and composed a refutation of schismatic teachers. He was particularly successful in writing didactic religious works, composing them either in the form of didactic verses or in the form of direct sermons. Polotsky's works of this sort were many. The success that this talented monk realized in Moscow was unusual. His personal charm and the important connections that he had in Russian society made it possible for him not only to maintain his own well-being but to help other South Russians settle in Moscow. The reaction against Kievan learning did not harm Polotsky, although Slavinetsky has pointed out that as a Latinist, Polotsky "did know something in Latin, although in Greek he knew very little."

The time of this reaction against the "Latin" learning of the Kievans (that is, the last quarter of the seventeenth century) posed the question of replacing the cultural leadership of the South Russians with that of the Greeks. There was a moment in Russian life when Greek influence could have greatly increased, namely, during the period of Nikon's predominance, in the 1650's and 1660's. Given to strong passions and feelings, Nikon completely succumbed to Greek influence and carried out his ecclesiastical "innovations" on orders from the Greeks, adopting from them even the external trivia of ecclesiastical ceremony. "Although he made a proper decision when he decided to bring Russian ecclesiastical books, ceremonies and rites into strict conformity with the contemporary Greeks," says Professor N. F. Kapterev, "at the same time Nikon also adopted for us the Greek style of pulpit, the Greek bishop's crozier, Greek mantles and cowls and Greek music. He built monasteries on the Greek model and gave them Greek names. He indiscriminately drew all Greeks close to himself, listened to them and acted according to their instructions. Everywhere he put Greek authority in the forefront."[17]

The Muscovite government maintained the same subordinate and obedient attitude toward the Greeks even after Nikon's fall from favor, until Nikon's final condemnation. It appeared that the Greek heirarchy now enjoyed its greatest opportunity to subordinate Moscow to its cultural influence, to create its own schools there, to install its own teachers and to found its own presses to print books of worship, instead of printing them in Italy. But the Greeks did nothing of the sort. On the contrary, their influence in Moscow soon dwindled completely. There were two main reasons for this.

First, the Greeks lacked the knowledge and the ability to retain the authority they had acquired. Nikon's personal enthusiasm for the Greeks had allowed no room for criticism, and so the Russian people were at first silent. Nikon's fall from power loosed their tongues, while the conduct of the Greeks gave them much to use against them. Above all else, Russians began to portray the Greeks as morally inferior people who were ready to sell the truth and to sacrifice things that are sacred for the sake of lavish "alms," that is, subsidies and bribes. Suffice it to say that such representations were not groundless. Moreover, the Greek Orthodoxy in which Nikon had come to believe did not seduce others. Not only did Nikon's opponents, the schismatic teachers, refuse to believe in it, but those who were neutral in the struggle spoke of it with scepticism. One of the writers of this period says of the Greeks: "They have lost their piety because of the pressure brought to bear upon them by the infidels. They have become separated from the wonder-working icons and the relics of the saints by sending them all to Russia, and so their devotional life became empty."

Many strongly agreed with the feelings of the Russian monk, Arseny Sukhanov, who had visited the East. He had told the Greeks to their face that just as the Pope was not the head of the Church, so the Greeks were not the source of faith. If it were true that in earlier times the Greeks had been the only source of faith, that source had now dried up and they themselves were suffering from thirst. How could they now offer the entire world a drink from such a source? After their long contact with the Greek clergy in Nikon's time, the most that Russians were willing to admit was that the Greek church was as Orthodox as the Russian.

Secondly, the conviction prevailed in Russia that the Greeks did not have any special learning of their own and that in this respect they were superior in no essential way to learned Kievans and West Europeans. Moreover, Russians understood that even if the Greeks did have learned men, they had not acquired their learning in Greek countries, which were under the Turkish yoke, but in the Latin West, especially in Catholic Italy, where they received their scientific training and where their Greek books were printed. For this reason the Greeks were in just as much danger of "becoming Latinized" as were the South Russians in the schools they had established in the Catholic manner. For both the language of learning was not Greek, but Latin. If this were so, why should one learn from the Greeks, when it was simpler to learn from one's own Russian teacher? And why should one work to learn the Greek language, when the Latin language was just as necessary and of greater scientific use?

Even under these circumstances, if the Greeks had made a special effort to secure control of the schools of Moscow, they perhaps would have been able to consolidate themselves in Russia. But they made no such effort. The history of the Greek schools in Moscow during the seventeenth century reveals the sad picture of how all attempts by the Muscovite government to acquire teachers from the Greek East remained unsuccessful because of the lack of attention by Greek ecclesiastical authorities, or by the latter's inability to find people suited for the task. The Greek schools that had sprung up in Moscow inevitably closed because of the unfitness of their instructors, while the East regarded this phenomenon, which was so shameful to the Greeks, with indifference.

The Greeks even acquitted themselves poorly in the matter of founding a higher school of Orthodoxy in Moscow, a matter that was important to the entire Orthodox world. The plan for such a school, or academy, originated in a circle of learned Kievans, among Semen Polotsky and his disciples (especially Silvester Medvedev). Tsarevna Sophia's government sanctioned it in 1682, at a time when the reaction of the higher Muscovite clergy against the Kievan scholars as "Latinizers" was running high. To oppose their "Latin learning" the Patriarch Joachim attempted to create "Greek learning" in a special school that he established in 1679. His endeavors proved successful at the time (1685), and this Muscovite "academy" began to follow Greek, not Latin, learning. Instruction in the academy was entrusted to the Greek brothers Likhudy, who had been summoned from the East, while Kievans and their Muscovite disciples were removed from it.

It would seem that the enterprise had fallen squarely into the hands of the Greeks, and the Greeks had only not to spoil it. But spoil it they did. The nature of the Likhudy's teaching was not essentially different from "Latin" teaching, for they themselves had studied in Venice and had been doctors of the University of Padua. This was pointed out to the authorities by the Kievans and their disciples. They also subjected the quality of the Likhudy's teaching to criticism and found it lacking. The personal conduct of the Likhudys and their sons, which was far from being moral, provided still more grounds for charges. Even the Patriarch of Jerusalem, Dositheos, who had recommended the Likhudys to the Russian authorities, called attention to this.

Because of all these accusations, slanders and intrigues, the Likhudys fled from Moscow but were caught and returned. They were not reappointed to the academy but were made teachers of the Italian language. The academy gradually came into the hands of people of the "Latin teaching," disciples of the Kievan academy, who introduced into its management and operation procedures that had been established in Kiev since olden times and imparted to it their spirit and orientation.

Thus in the end the ecclesiastical education imported from the Ukraine was incorporated into Muscovite life.

The ecclesiastical education brought into Muscovy from the Ukraine was invested with the outward forms of Polish culture; inevitably it had to become a source of Polish influence upon the Muscovites. And so it did. We do not mean those surface borrowings that found their way into the Muscovite way of life through common, everyday contact. Moscow always saw enough of this sort of borrowing. In Muscovite stalls one could always buy Polish soap, Polish mittens and caps and other items of "Polish workmanship" or Polish fashion. Apart from this sort of adoption the upper levels of the Muscovite populace began to accept, in addition to theological learning, the Polish language and the taste for Polish literature common among the South Russian teachers. They also began to adopt Polish customs and Polish dress.

The Polish vogue infected the Kremlin palace itself. Semen Polotsky's pupil, Tsar Feodor Alexeevich, was well disposed toward Polish novelties. He had mastered the Polish language and, according to the testimony of contemporaries, read books "not only in our language, but in the Polish language." He also loved Polish dress, Polish music and tunes. The boiars acquired a taste for "insignia" (coats of arms) and genealogical tables of a rather fantastic nature, as well as for portraits and icons done in the Polish manner by Polish painters. Some boiars adopted Polish livery for their menials and themselves loved to dress in Polish costumes, "wearing sabers at their side and Polish surcoats." Large numbers of Polish books appeared in their libraries. Translations from the Polish or from Latin works of Polish literature greatly increased, from serious works to novels and scabrous "facetiae" and "anecdotes." In short, new things done "in the Polish manner" began to rival the new things of the Germans.

V *Peter the Great in Relation to the Cultural Setting of His Day*

We now stand on the threshold of Peter the Great's so-called "era of reforms." At the moment that Peter assumed control of the state, that state had accepted much that was new and much that had been acquired from foreigners. The state lived under the cultural influence of foreigners and felt the pressure of their money. People who still held the old Muscovite outlook sensed that "the entire world was reeling," and it was necessary to save the "Rus of old." But the practical managers of Russian policy were convinced that the "Rus of old" had to be changed. They thought that "for a good man there is no shame in borrowing from abroad, from foreigners, even from your enemies." In the well known words of S. M. Soloviev, "the need to move along a new path was acknowledged . . . . The people arose and were ready to move . . . . They awaited a leader, and that leader appeared." This was Peter.[18]

What was Peter's relation to the world in which he lived, and what constitutes his historical role? Must we follow the old view of Chaadaev, which maintains that Peter repudiated ancient Russia before the entire world and dug a chasm between our past and our present? Or shall we adopt Paul Miliukov's later view, according to which Peter did not play the guiding role in his own reforms and, as Catherine II rashly put it, "did not know himself what laws had to be instituted for the good of the state." According to Miliukov's opinion of Peter's state reform, "this reform, which was prepared spontaneously and debated collectively, . . . penetrated into his consciousness only at secondhand and in chance fragments. Life raised the problems. More or less capable and skillful people formulated the solutions. The Tsar occasionally caught the main idea of a suggestion or (and perhaps more often) grasped its practical application."

To answer the questions we have posed, we must first determine how Peter's personality was formed and what were the cultural influences of his childhood and youth.

The family political intrigues amid which Peter had to grow up are well recorded. Aroused by palace conspirators, the *streltsy* regiments of the Moscow garrison in May, 1682 organized bloody reprisals against some of the boiar circles in the palace and city. We can say that Peter's first conscious impression, in his tenth year, was of this massacre, which was provoked by the hostility of Tsar Alexis' older children toward their stepmother (Peter's mother) and her relatives. In the days of this mutiny Peter and his mother were surrounded by *streltsy*, who in their presence tortured and murdered their relatives and the boiars. With his own eyes Peter saw the blood and tortures, trembled with terror amid the throng of *streltsy* and awaited death at their hands. Many years later he confessed that the mere recollection of the *streltsy* made him tremble all over. "I cannot sleep when I think of it," he said.

The days of the mutiny were agonizing - three long days of murder and violence. But the time that followed was no less agonizing. During the entire summer and fall of 1682 the *streltsy* were in ferment. For this reason the royal family left Moscow and in their anxiety wandered about the monasteries and summer residences around the capital. Besides defending her son from the *streltsy*, Natalia Kirillovna had to protect him from other evils that were close at hand - his sister Sophia and Sophia's relatives, the Miloslavsky family. Though he wore the royal cloth, the lad lived in constant fear. His accession brought him not power and respect, but horrors and woe. When Sophia, who had seized power, thought that they could return to the palace in Moscow because the *streltsy* had been pacified, understandably Peter and his mother returned unwillingly. The chambers and rooms of the Kremlin terrified the young Tsar. They had been flooded with blood that had been dear to him. He was frightened to live in them and feared open and secret enemies.

These things are worth considering thoroughly for an understanding of why Peter never loved the Kremlin and why he hated the *streltsy*. He and his mother preferred to live in the summer residences near Moscow and visited the city only when necessary. Moscow, the Kremlin palace and the people of the court had become alien and obnoxious to Peter. With a cold heart he regarded those majestic rooms in which his father and grandfather had lived and in which all their state work had been concentrated. Old Moscow was not at all dear to Peter.

Seven years passed, and matters between Peter and Sophia came to an open break. In August, 1689 Peter experienced a new attack of terror. He was then living in the village of Preobrazhenskoe in the environs of Moscow. He received word one night that *streltsy* sent from Moscow by Sophia were coming to kill him and that he had better escape. In fright, Peter rushed to the formidable Trinity-St. Sergius

Monastery, dashing from his palace before he had finished dressing. Later some official reports said of him that he "had gone on a quick trip in only his night-shirt." Others added that "the Tsar was driven away from Preobrazhenskoe barefoot and in his night-shirt alone." It is true that Sophia did not admit that she had sent the *streltsy* against her brother. The *diak* Shaklovity, who commanded the *streltsy*, also denied any attempt upon Peter. "He became frantic and fled of his own accord," he later said with vexation of Peter. But even if we allow that Peter had been frightened away for no reason, he had nonetheless suffered some difficult moments and became still more embittered against the old Muscovite order.

The *streltsy* incurred severe punishment; Shaklovity was put to death; Sophia was forced to leave the government and reside in a monastery. The state passed into Peter's hands. But this did not end the turmoil in Moscow. Ten years later another mutiny of the *streltsy* broke out, while Peter was abroad. Peter hurriedly returned to Moscow in August, 1698 and carried out a terrible "investigation" of the *streltsy*, with hundreds of tortures and executions, and completely destroyed the *streltsy* forces. With extraordinary cruelty Peter spilled whole rivers of blood, for he considered this the only way to deal with his enemies.

This is how Peter was influenced by the circumstances of his childhood and youth. This series of dangers shook his nerve; it fostered in him a hatred for Muscovite institutions and a cruelty toward people who were inimical to him. It shattered the peace and harmony of his family. In short, it deprived him of the serene happiness and quiet joys of early youth. The beginning of Peter's life was very unhappy and ruined his health and his character.

Moreover, Peter's unhappy childhood interfered with his regular education and training. While the young Peter lived with his mother in the chambers of the Russian palace, his life proceeded according to the customary ceremonial of the court. Surrounded by nannies and later by male nurses and "lads," with whom he "amused himself," Peter spent his time in games of a military nature. His attendants were constantly preparing or purchasing for the Tsarevich toy bows, banners (standards), little drums, little gilded cannons, wooden guns (carbines and arquebuses), small battle axes and sabers.

At the age of five Peter was exposed to learning. The *diak* Zotov began to teach him the alphabet and spelling and, according to the ancient custom, he read and studied with the Tsarevich the Prayer Book, then the Psalter, then the Acts and the Gospels. Then Peter began to write himself. He read and remembered well, but wrote poorly. "Nothing could be more hideous than his handwriting," said one scholar who concerned himself with Peter's manuscripts.

Whether Peter at this time studied arithmetic ("figures") is not known with certainty. The custom of the time dictated that, after reading and writing, one had to pursue "grammatical" studies. A learned monk would have to join the Tsarevich and with him begin to study the scholastic science of that time, namely, the Latin language, poetics, rhetoric and theology. In this manner the older brothers (and even sisters) of the Tsarevich had studied, under the direction of Semen Polotsky, who was a model representative of contemporary scholastic knowledge. Peter himself also had to study in the same manner.

But when the mutiny of the *streltsy* erupted, there could no longer be any question of monastic learning. Sophia did not think of educating her unloved brother. And Tsaritsa Natalia Kirillovna had no desire at all to permit learned monks with her son. During those years they "adhered" to Sophia and the Miloslavsky family and took their side. Therefore the Tsaritsa considered them dangerous enemies. For these reasons Peter remained a superficial dabbler and did not experience the influence of the theological and scholastic knowledge that was deemed necessary for an educated Orthodox person.

Left without knowledge, the youth found pastimes and work for himself. The summer residences (with the exception of Kolomenskoe alone) were in no way reminiscent of the Kremlin palace. Instead of imposing stone buildings and palaces, ordinary, though very spacious wooden houses were used as residences during the royal sojourn there, and these could not possibly accommodate a large retinue. Instead of throngs of eminent courtiers, a small number of simple servants were employed here. Instead of the squares and courts that were "behind bars" in the Kremlin, the summer residences were surrounded by flower and vegetable gardens, and beyond them were spacious fields and

Second Half of the Seventeenth Century

groves. Next to the summer estates stood the simple villages of the crown peasants. In his own villages of Preobrazhenskoe or Izmailovo the young Tsar lived not as a sovereign but as a landowner.

He made ample use of the spaciousness and simplicity of this rural setting. With household youths and young servants - the "Preobrazhenskoe stablemen," as they were called in Moscow - Peter created for himself a special, noisy and merry life. He now occupied himself with military games, as he had earlier done in Moscow. From his "stablemen" he formed "regiments," named for the villages where they were located: the Preobrazhensky and the Semenovsky. These comprised a small "playmate" company, with which the Tsar played at war in the spaciousness of the countryside. Around the village of Preobrazhenskoe Peter built for himself a "play fortress," with the name of Pressburg, armed it with cannon and began his "service" there, imitating real military procedures in everything he did. Little by little this "amusement" acquired the aspect of serious business, and Peter, in his enthusiasm for it, began to learn what a military man had to know. Between noisy amusements he sat down with a German teacher for "figures" and practiced the four rules of arithmetic, calling them in Latin *"aditsia, supstraktsia, multoplikatsia, divizia."* Having mastered them, he proceeded to geometry and fortification, in order to learn how to erect fortress walls, how to measure distance with an astrolabe or how to determine "how far a bomb will fly, when you wish to shoot at an enemy place." It was fun to learn all these entertaining "bits of wisdom," for this knowledge could immediately be put into practice.

Thus from these childhood games, which were not restricted by the confinement of a town and the rigorous procedures of a large palace, Peter grew in his love for exact and practical (applied) knowledge. Without realizing it, Peter prepared himself to become a mathematician and technician, whereas his brothers and sisters had all been educated as theologians.

If in those days Russians had to turn to learned Greeks and Little Russian monks for theological knowledge, for technical instruction they had to go to the foreigners from Western Europe. Almost adjacent to the village of Preobrazhenskoe stood the large German settlement, in which the military and commercial foreigners lived. As soon as Peter became interested in military science, he turned to the foreigners of this settlement. From there he procured his teachers of mathematics and military science. From there experts in "ship architecture" came to him and taught him to build ships and navigate with sails. Finally, it was from that source that he acquired his knowledge of foreign languages - Dutch and German.

Since the days of Tsar Alexis, Peter's whole family had been accustomed to using the knowledge and services of foreigners. But none of them had become so attached to these foreigners as Peter. He not only drew them close to himself in his amusements and work, but also established close and friendly familiarity with them. He went to them in their settlement and visited their homes and churches. He learned and amused himself in their midst. He danced at their parties and reveled at their carouses.

While some foreigners were influencing Peter for the better, others were ruining and corrupting him. Patrick Gordon, whom we know, was always Peter's diligent teacher and adviser. The Swiss, Franz Lefort, who was promoted to the rank of general by Peter and in time became Peter's friend, was useful to him in many ways, but caused Peter no little harm through his revels and debauchery. Under the influence of his foreign friends the young Tsar began to depart from the ancient customs of Russian life and "became a Mahometan," as Russians used to say. It was said of him that he had "wandered away into amusements, was abandoning the better things and was beginning to create everything sad and grievous." "The Sovereign does not honor himself, but dishonors his own person," others added, condemning Peter's conduct.

Such was the result of the wholly unforeseen and unexpected circumstances that formed Peter's character. His isolation from the traditions of the court and the old mentality of court life, his lack of "knowledge," his unusual manners (which clashed with the ceremonies that were practiced by traditional Russians), his open inclination to side with the Western Europeans because of their technology and military science, and his complete freedom from the influence of Kievan and Greek scholasticism - these were the characteristic traits of the young

Second Half of the Seventeenth Century 139

Peter. He was a new type in the royal family, an unprecedented cultural phenomenon at the apex of Russian society.

It cost Peter nothing to tear himself away from the olden times, for he chanced to grow up apart from the ancient way of life and could not value it at all. On the contrary, his personal hatred of Sophia and her family, the Miloslavsky clan, caused Peter to hate the palace in which Sophia had lived and ruled, the troops upon which she had depended and the administration with whose help she had acted. Peter was inclined to identify Sophia's court faction with the entire government, indeed the entire Muscovite system. Because he did not value the old, he not only sacrificed it lightly for new forms of life and authority but often condemned and persecuted the old with animosity. This mentality, which was born of personal hostility, invested Peter's activities with a sharp, stormy and openly revolutionary character, although in reality Peter did not intend a general political or social revolution and was not trying to create any sort of "abyss" between old and new Russia.

Wielding all the fullness of autocratic power and with an excessive love of power, Peter merely gave rein to the inclinations formed during his childhood and the views created by the circumstances of his youth. Foreign influences became unusually strong and Western European forms of life became the official model for Russia's ruling circles, because from his childhood the Tsar had been accustomed to them and enamored of them. The South Russian and Greek monks were restricted to their special realm of church administration and teaching, because the palace of the new Tsar was not interested in their learning, nor their orations and verses, except at times of church holidays and parades. The defenders of "the Rus of old," that is, of the old fiction that Russia was a superior nation and one chosen by God, were regarded as a dangerous faction of opposition and lived in fear of repression. All this constituted Peter's cultural reform.

It was more a matter of consciousness than of principle. Peter knew what he wanted, but he was a practical man, not a theoretician. He did not elevate to the realm of abstract principle that which he undertook for the good of the state and the enlightenment of the public. He did not draw up nor did he accept from abroad sweeping utopian plans for reform, for which "the hand of wisdom would mark the hours of prosperity" of his monarchy. By promoting foreign influence and arranging the machinery of government "in the Dutch manner" or "in the Swedish manner," he knew that the result would be the transplanting of Western European institutions to Russian soil and the cultural rapprochement of Russia and Europe. And for this he worked purposefully and with full consciousness, as his own manuscripts document.

He did not receive the idea for one or another measure secondhandedly, as Miliukov thinks, but created and polished the text of his laws with his own hands, just as their ideas and forms matured in his mind. One of the experts on the Petrine era, who passed away too young, in arguing with Miliukov's view, has correctly written:

> It is clearly evident from the many documents written in Peter's own hand and now published that he was not only a seafarer and carpenter, an expert on ships and a turner, but that he also spent long hours at his desk. His many letters (written for the most part in his own hand) from the first half of his reign indicate that he was not lost in details, but actively directed all the vast work of outfitting the army and defending the country, while his continual and persistent reminders stimulated the energies of his senators and generals. In the second half of his reign Peter worked on legislative matters with the same inexhaustible energy as he had worked with his axe in the shipyards. Peter worked on maritime law for five months, for four days each week, from five in the morning until noon and from four in the afternoon to eleven o'clock at night. The greater part of the manuscripts of these regulations is written in his hand, while the remainder is sprinkled with his corrections. Rarely has an editorial staff seen such a stylist as Peter. In the Senate archives are preserved rough notebooks of statutes of the colleges. They contain lengthy insertions and very many corrections in the Tsar's handwriting. A significant part of Peter's decrees, for instance, such edicts as those concerning the right of primogeniture and the duties of the Procurator General, were elaborated by Peter himself. Peter

accepted only the first paragraph of the draft of the decree that was submitted to him on the duties of the Procurator General. The remaining eleven he composed himself. Four times the draft of the decree was rewritten by clerks of the Cabinet, and each time it was sprinkled with Peter's new corrections. From these corrections it can be seen that Peter abandoned almost entirely the original draft prepared by others and gradually worked out the law on the office of the Procurator, which became one of the cornerstones of the Petrine Senate.[19]

This comment, by an historian who is not inclined to idealize Peter and who knew this era very well, firmly establishes Peter's competence and conscientiousness.

Finding his country exposed to various cultural influences, Peter gave full play to one of them and devoted all his powers to its final triumph. We now understand why he chose this one and how he labored on its behalf.

NOTES TO THE INTRODUCTION

1. The most comprehensive survey of early Russian relations with the West is to be found in V. T. Pashuto, *Vneshnaia politika drevnei Rusi* (Moscow, 1968). Many interesting details are also contained in George Vernadsky, *Kievan Russia (History of Russia*, Vol. II), New Haven, 1949.

2. Vernadsky, *op. cit.; Russia at the Dawn of the Modern Age (History of Russia*, Vol. IV), New Haven, 1959, p. 80.

3. Dmitry Tschizhevsky (Dmitrij Cizevskij), *A History of Russian Literature From the XI Century to the Baroque* (S.-Gravenhage, 1956), pp. 145-229.

4. The English edition is John T. Alexander (trans.), *The Time of Troubles. A Historical Study of the Internal Crisis and Social Struggle in 16th and 17th Century Muscovy* (Lawrence, Kansas, 1970).

5. S. F. Platonov, *Lektsii po russkoi istorii* (9th ed., Petrograd, 1915), pp. 675-678. The abridged and not fully satisfactory English translation of Platonov's *History of Russia* was published in 1928 (edited by Frank A. Golder) and reissued (1964, 1969) by University Prints and Reprints (now Academic International, Hattiesburg, Mississippi).

6. *Sovetskaia istoricheskaia entsiklopediia*, Vol. XI (Moscow, 1968), col. 203-204; also M. V. Nechkina, ed., *Ocherki istorii*

istoricheskoi nauki v SSSR. Vol. III (Moscow, 1963), pp. 271-272, 316-318.

7. G. V. Vernadsky, "Iz vospominanii," *Novy zhurnal,* Vol. 100 (New York, 1970), pp. 211-221.

8. Reminiscences of Vladimir V. Weidlé as told to the writer of these lines in November, 1970 in Washington, D. C.

NOTES TO THE TEXT

Chapter One

THE SIXTEENTH CENTURY AND TIME OF TROUBLES

1. Nicholas Poppel's offer of a crown to Ivan III was intended as a preamble to a military alliance between Muscovy and the Holy Roman Empire. It was a point of Western medieval political theory that the Holy Roman Emperor, as the descendant of the Roman Caesars, could alone award Christian princes political titles. Platonov's subsequent references to "Caesar" intend, of course, the Western emperor.

2. Sophia Paleologos was the niece of the last Byzantine emperor, Constantine XI, who had died defending Constantinople from the Turks in 1453. Although she had accepted Catholicism and had become a ward of the Pope in Rome, she converted to Orthodoxy upon her marriage to Ivan III in 1472.

3. For an account of Contarini's travels and residence in Moscow, see *Travels to Tana and Persia by Josafa Barbaro and Ambrogio Contarini* (London: The Hakluyt Society, 1873).

4. The Russian people called foreigners from Northern and Western Europe "Germans" *(nemtsy)*. The word apparently derives from the Russian *nemoi* (mute), and was used originally to characterize those unable to speak the Russian language.

5. When the city was burned by the invading Tatars these Englishmen had sought refuge in a cellar and died when the structure above them caught fire.

6. The Stroganov family, one of the richest in Russia, engaged in commercial and mining activities. They were also responsible for beginning the conquest and colonization of Siberia.

7. The oprichnina was a special institution created by Ivan IV to weaken the power of the aristocracy and offset their real or potential opposition to him. Ivan set aside part of the state as his own personal domain, which he ruled in autocratic fashion. His chosen officials in this domain, the oprichniki, served as a secret police and arrested and executed dissident aristocrats and other malcontents.

8. Every sixth of January the Tsar, accompanied by his chief advisers and high officials would join high ecclesiastical dignitaries on the banks of the Moscow River for the "Jordan ceremony," or blessing of the waters.

9. Sir Jerome Horsey lived in Russia almost constantly from 1573 in the service of the English Russian Company, until his expulsion in 1590. His work, *The Travels of Sir Jerome Horsey,* (London, 1856), is an account of his life there and his missions on behalf of the Company.

10. Horsey was the first to offer this contention, which was later accepted by the Russian historian, Karamzin. Later scholars, however, deny Bomel's influence upon the Tsar in this respect. For particulars on Bomel, see J. Hamel, *England and Russia, Comprising the Voyages of John Tradescant the Elder, Sir Hugh Willoughby, Richard Chancellor, Nelson, and Others to the White Sea* (London, 1854), pp. 202-206.

11. Russians generally regarded the beard as an essential tribute of the Christian, in imitation of Christ and the saints portrayed on icons, all of whom were bearded.

12. Ivan the Terrible had the custom of expressing his goodwill and

kindness in this manner. Thus, for example, in 1570 he patted Duke Magnus at the end of an audience, slapped him on the shoulder and assured him of his affection for Germans. This was officially recorded with the words: "He placed his hand upon him and was gracious to him." (Platonov's note)

13. The booklet by Professor V. I. Savva, *Neskol'ko sluchaev izucheniia inostrannykh iazykov russkimi liud'mi vo vtoroi polovine XVI veka* (Kharkov, 1913), discusses the dispatch and travel of Russians abroad for language study. The majority were sent to the East to study the Greek language. Trips to the West, it seems, were then still very rare. (Platonov's note)

14. A Frenchman who joined the Russian service as a commander of cavalry in 1601 and later served the first Pretender, believing him authentic.

15. The word "Kokui" probably derives from the Russian word for headband or headdress and was used in reference to the unfamiliar dress of the foreigners.

16. The *strigol'niki* (Shearers) appeared in Novgorod and Pskov at the end of the fourteenth century and denied such traditional Christian dogma as prayer for the dead, the efficacy of sacraments and the need for an established ecclesiastical hierarchy. Their leaders were executed.

17. The "Judaizers" appeared in northwest Russia, chiefly in Novgorod, in the fifteenth century and followed the kabbala, practiced astrology, denounced the corruption of the Russian Church and repeated many of the theological contentions of the strigol'niki. Their leaders were burned at the stake in 1504.

18. We have chosen these citations from M. N. Speransky's most interesting essay, "Ideinye dvizheniia v staroi Moskve," which appeared in the collection, *Moskva v ee proshlom i*

Notes to the Text

nastoiashchem, II, vyp. 4, printed by the Obrazovanie publishing house. (Platonov's note)

19. Interesting data concerning these Russian youths abroad is presented in the work of N. V. Golitsyn, "Nauchno-obrazovatel'nye snosheniia Rossii s zapadom v nachale XVII veka," *Chteniia v obshchestve istorii i drevnostei* (1898). (Platonov's note)

20. But the Pole Niemojewski, who saw these two units in formation during Marina Mniszech's arrival in Moscow, recalled them with scorn. In his words, they wore poor caftans. Some had swords and boots, while others had Cossack sabers and high-heeled shoes. "In fact, one could see that these artisans (i. e., they were hardly knights) were all trash." Their commander, Knutsen, was from Denmark and had belonged to the retinue of Duke Hans, who died in Moscow. (Platonov's note)

21. Another eyewitness counted thirty-six dappled horses attached to the carriage (in Polish the color of these horses was conveyed by the word *tarentowatych).* A third eyewitness saw only eight dappled horses with red tails and crests. (Platonov's note)

22. The people of Moscow did not yet know that Dimitry had accepted the Catholic faith. Hence, Marina's baptism into Orthodoxy was the immediate concern.

23. Suffice it to say that Pan Martin Stadnicki was one of the most eminent Poles in Moscow. During Marina Mniszech's march to the Russian capital he had been invested with "full power over the management of the court of Her Majesty, the Tsarina, and the post of marshal of her court." (Platonov's note)

24. According to neutral testimony supplied by the German, Paerle, the Polish ambassadors had demanded that they be given easy chairs in church during the Pretender's coronation. When the

Pretender refused this, they went to one side and sat down anyway. (Platonov's note)

25. The Germans report other figures: Bussow - 2,135 men; Petrei - 1,702; Margeret gives almost the same figure - 1,705. Massa says 1,500. (Platonov's note)

26. Ivan Bolotnikov, a runaway slave, launched a social revolution among the Cossacks. His forces marched on Moscow and besieged the city in 1606. When his army was defeated by Shuisky in 1607 Bolotnikov was executed along with other leaders of his movement.

27. Russians called the area that had formerly constituted the Khanate of Kazan (which Ivan IV conquered from the Tatars and incorporated into the Muscovite state) the "Lower Reaches."

28. Prince Dimitry Pozharsky commanded the Russian army of liberation that drove the Poles from Moscow in 1612.

Chapter Two

FIRST HALF OF THE SEVENTEENTH CENTURY

1. Whence his Russian name - Ivan Ul'ianov. (Platonov's note) The Russian name Ivan is the equivalent of the English John. Ul'ianov derives from the English name William.

2. Alexander Lisowski, an exile from Lithuania, recruited a force of 30,000 survivors of the army that had served Bolotnikov and sided with the second Pretender. His forces were responsible for the siege and devastation of the Trinity Monastery that Platonov mentions below.

3. V. D. Tsvetaev, *Protestantstvo i protestanty v Rossii do epokhi preobrazovanii* (Moscow, 1890), p. 249. (Platonov's note)

4. Gramotin had another family name, Kurbatov. Russians had the habit of not being content with their family names and of adding to them or substituting names formed from a nickname or the patronymic of one's father. Thus Prince Ivan Andreevich Khvorostinin, whom we shall mention below, was called Khvorostinin-Starkov, inasmuch as his father's nickname was "Starko." The Koshkin family changed its last name with each generation (Zakharin, Yuriev, Romanov) according to the first name of their grandfather. (Platonov's note)

5. Here is an excerpt from one of Gramotin's letters to the Lithuanian chancellor, Sapieha, in September of 1610: "Thanks to your kindness I have reached Moscow in good health, and

because of the King's commands and your graciousness everything has turned out well.... In Moscow the Patriarch and all churchmen, as well as the boiars and people of all classes, recognized the prince as their sovereign and kissed the cross. May everything turn out well. As far as other matters are concerned, I discussed them in detail with the honorable elder Pan Gosiewski. I beg Your Grace to command me to serve you, Your Grace, and I shall be very happy to do so." (Platonov's note)

6. According to the old definition, the cup-bearer *(kravchii)* "supervised everything that had to do with the sovereign's table, such as the dishes, beverages, table linens, etc. He stood at the table while the sovereign ate and on especially festive or ceremonious occasions stood directly opposite the sovereign and cut and served his food." In Dal's dictionary the word *kravchii* or *kraichii* is said to come from the word "to cut"; hence, "one who cuts roasts and pies at the table." (Platonov's note)

7. When Moscow was in danger of coming directly under the rule of King Sigismund III of Poland, Patriarch Hermogen roused the Russian people to the danger of enslavement by Poland. His agitation is usually credited with creating the great upsurge of nationalistic feeling among the Russians that in time was to drive the Poles from Moscow.

8. Martin Czechowicz and Simon Budny were important for introducing some of the more rationalistic and sectarian ideas of the Reformation to Poland. Budny had been especially interested in converting Russian Orthodox clergymen to Protestantism.

9. Socinianism, a school of thought founded by Faustus and Laelius Socinus, denied the divinity of Christ, the Trinity, original sin and other traditional Christian beliefs. The radical sect won many followers along Russia's western borders.

10. A. Golubtsov, *Preniia o vere, vyzvannye delom korolevicha*

Vol'demara i tsarevny Irinny Mikhailovny (Moscow, 1891), chapter III. D. Tsvetaev, *Literaturnaia bor'ba s protestantstvom v Moskovskom gosudarstve* (Moscow, 1887), chapter III. (Platonov's note)

11. The *Margariti* and *Zlatostrui* were compilations of homilies and other selections from the writings of St. John Chrysostom and other Fathers of the Church.

12. When the Russian people heeded the appeals of Patriarch Hermogen and in March, 1611 besieged the Polish garrison of Moscow in the Kremlin, parts of Moscow were set afire by the Poles to hinder Russian operations against them. The blaze spread throughout the city and engulfed much of it, leaving thousands homeless and destitute.

13. In 1551 a council of the Russian church was convened to eradicate abuses in ecclesiastical life. It was later known as the council of the "Hundred Chapters" because its pronouncement on church reforms were issued in a document divided into one hundred articles.

14. Filaret Romanov had opposed the installation of Sigismund of Poland as Tsar of Moscow. He was arrested by the Polish forces in Moscow and deported to Poland, where he remained in captivity until 1619. During the reign of Shuisky he had been appointed Patriarch of Moscow.

15. We need not describe exactly what led to Dionisius' accusal and arrest. Suffice it to say that his main guilt consisted in removing two words, "and fire," from the Prayer Book in the prayer for the blessing of the waters (January 6) and for his statement that the ritual of dipping a burning candle into blessed water was incorrect. He also excluded from the liturgy two prayers in which "the priest absolves himself" of sin ("for it was ludicrous that he should forgive his own sins," Arseny Glukhoi observed). (Platonov's note)

16. Until 1564 only the Archbishop of Novgorod had enjoyed the privilege of wearing a white monastic cowl. In that year Tsar Ivan IV bestowed this right also upon the Metropolitan of Moscow. By Dionisius' day the white cowl had become a symbol of respect and recognition that was conferred only upon eminent churchmen.

17. Maxim the Greek had been recruited for service in Moscow in 1518 from Italy, where he had studied under the famous and unfortunate Savonarola. In Moscow he translated ecclesiastical works into Slavonic and corrected earlier translations. Because he did not know Slavonic, Maxim had to translate into Latin, from which his assistants rendered his versions into Slavonic. Mistakes inevitably occurred, and Maxim was accused of heresy and sentenced to perpetual residence in Russian monasteries until his death in 1551.

18. Stefan Vonifatiev was the confessor of Tsar Alexis and close associate and friend of Patriarch Nikon. Vonifatiev created a circle of sympathizers who sponsored religious renewal in Russia by promoting popular devotions, canonizing new Russian saints, closing taverns and other disreputable establishments and the like. He was especially hated by foreigners for his insistence that Tsar Alexis legislate against the hiring of Russians by foreign merchants.

19. Although Neronov also believed that reforms in the Russian church were needed, he reproached Nikon for accepting the authority of foreigners in his renovations. He accused Nikon of teaching that the Greeks and Ukrainians were in error and apostasy, even while Nikon relied upon their practices and interpretations in his own programs.

20. The Russian church taught that no man should marry more than three times.

21. Shakhovskoi meant, of course, that the Russian church should

Notes to the Text

recognize Waldemar's earlier baptism and not repeat the sacrament with the immersions customary among the Russians.

22. This letter has come down to us in the form of a memorandum to Tsar Michael Feodorovich. It is very verbose and ornate but very prudent and contains nothing that is heretical. (Platonov's note)

23. The "Frozen Sea" was the name by which Russians knew the Barents Sea.

Chapter Three

SECOND HALF OF THE SEVENTEENTH CENTURY

1. In times of crisis the Muscovite government could order the provincial gentry to leave their individual estates and assemble in military or administrative units. This state service was rendered in return for grants of land, or estates.

2. The *Ulozhenie* (Code) of 1648-49 was an attempt to provide a codification of all the laws of the realm and to standardize legal practices throughout the state.

3. We have spoken of this earlier. On Tsar Alexis' concern about security troops, see the interesting remarks of A. I. Zaozersky, in his work *Tsar Aleksei Mikhailovich v svoem khoziaistve* (St. Petersburg, 1917), p. 334ff. (Platonov's note)

4. See Kliuchevsky, *Kurs russkoi istorii,* III, lectures 56 and 57; I. P. Kozlovsky, *F. M. Rtishchev* (Kiev, 1906); N. N. Kashkin, *Rodoslovnye razvedki,* I (1912), pp. 402-449 (which is a detailed biography of F. M. Rtishchev); E. A. Likhach, *Blizhnii boiarin A. L. Ordin-Nashchokin* (St. Petersburg, 1904), a reprint from *Russkii biograficheskii slovar';* V. S. Ikonnikov's article on Ordin-Nashchokin in *Russkaia starina,* X-XI (1882). Detailed bibliographies are provided by Kashkin and Likhach. (Platonov's note)

5. Avvakum was the leader of the schismatics who opposed Nikon's reforms. He became such a great enemy of the established church that he was ordered burned at the stake in 1682.

Notes to the Text 155

6. Yury Krizhanich was a Croatian Catholic priest who apparently undertook a personal mission to Moscow, in order to unite the Orthodox and Catholic churches. Exiled to Siberia for reasons still not fully understood, Krizhanich composed a political tract for Tsar Alexis and his advisers, in which he urged the unification of all Slavic peoples under Russian protection.

7. It is interesting that Nashchokin implemented his ideas about new forms of urban self-government precisely in Pskov, where he was voevoda in 1665. To develop local autonomy he reformed the popular institutions of Pskov "according to the example of foreign lands." He hoped that in this respect Pskov would serve as an example for other Russian towns. But his experiment was unsuccessful, largely because the people of Pskov constantly quarreled among themselves. (Platonov's note)

8. Throughout his career as chancellor Nashchokin suffered the opposition and enmity of the Russian boiars, who considered him an outsider because of his humble origins.

9. V. O. Kliuchevsky, *Kurs russkoi istorii,* III, lecture 58, pp. 459-460. (Platonov's note)

10. Kotoshikhin's *O Rossii v tsarstvovanie Alekseia Mikhailovicha* (4th ed., 1906), p. 54. (Platonov's note)

11. The *gostinaia sotnia* ("merchants' hundred") was the administrative body in which merchants were grouped, usually in numbers of one hundred, for rendering special service, such as military duty in times of crisis, to the state.

12. It is interesting to observe that according to the official "list of estimates" of 1632 the foreign cavalry and infantry units of the Russian army numbered 6,118 men under 105 foreign officers. Thus in half a century the regular Russian army increased in numbers by fifteen times, while at almost the same time the

number of foreign officers grew by ten times. In 1663 (according to E. Stashevsky's calculations) there were 55,714 men in the regular units, commanded by 2,422 "people who gave orders." But how many of this number were foreign officers is undetermined. (Platonov's note)

13. A. Brückner, *Patrik Gordon i ego dnevnik* (St. Petersburg, 1878), p. 45. Gordon's memorandum is reproduced in full in his diary. (Platonov's note)

14. Thus in 1630 Tsar Michael's brother-in-law, Prince I. M. Katyrev-Rostovsky, requested in a special petition that the Tsar give him for his headache medicine "from your royal apothecary, from your royal oils." Similar requests are also known. (Platonov's note)

15. This is how medical specialization was distinguished in Moscow. It was said that "this is a matter for a doctor, and not for a surgeon, because the disease in internal." But "he has an external disease, sores on his left leg, so this is a matter for a surgeon, not a doctor." (Platonov's note)

16. Muscovite theologians had clashed with the Ukrainians over the question of the Eucharist. Ukrainian theologians had attempted to explain the mystery of the Eucharist by using the western Thomistic distinction of substance and accidents. To Muscovite minds, the entire notion that reason could be applied to the formulation of theological beliefs was alien. Any rational development of dogma was considered heretical.

17. N. F. Kapterev, *Kharakter otnoshenii Rossii k pravoslavnomu Vostoku v XVI i XVII stoletiiakh* (1914), 2nd ed., p. 444. The last chapter of this work is an excellent outline of how the Greeks declined in importance in Russia during the seventeenth and eighteenth centuries. (Platonov's note)

18. *Sobranie sochinenii S. M. Solovieva,* p. 1001. (Platonov's note)

19. This passage is taken from the interesting article by N. P. Pavlov-Sil'vansky, "Ob istoricheskom samounizhenii," *S.-Peterburgskie vedomosti* (September 10, 1901), no. 248. The article was signed with the pseudonym, "Lesovik." (Platonov's note)

GLOSSARY

Aptekarskii prikaz (Aptekarskaia palata) - The department of the Muscovite government that regulated medical affairs of the court, oversaw the maintenance and use of medicines or drugs and directed the affairs of Russian and foreign physicians.

archimandrite - Head or abbot of a prominent monastery.

boiar - Nobleman of the highest rank of the Muscovite service aristocracy. This title could be conferred only by the Tsar.

boiar duma - The council of prominent service noblemen. It assisted the Tsar in matters of legislation, administration and foreign affairs. It was abolished by Peter I about 1700.

Cossacks - Frontier settlers in Muscovy. Usually renegades or refugees from Muscovy and Lithuania, they formed autonomous communities along the Don, Dnieper and Ural rivers. Only occasionally did they recognize the authority of the central Muscovite government.

deti boiarskie - Literally, sons of the boiars. They were a lower echelon of service noblemen in Muscovy who comprised the largest class of military servitors.

diak (plural, diaki) - State secretary. They served as assistants to the boiars, performed as officials in various departments and at times were appointed heads of government departments. In the 17th century they numbered about one hundred. They have been called the "mainspring of the Moscow bureaucratic apparatus."

gostinyi dvor (plural, gostinye dvory) - Square where foreign merchants maintained their shops and stalls. Also used to denote a large court or hall containing commercial shops or stalls.

gost' (plural, gosti) - Richest, highest and most privileged rank of merchants. They received this title from the Tsar and served the government by collecting state revenue and regulating state commercial operations. They numbered as few as thirty men.

Kitaigorod - The "Walled City" section of Moscow, directly east of the Kremlin. Its name derives from baskets, known as *kit*, which were filled with earth and used to reinforce the wall that surrounded this section. Here foreign merchants and traders from other Russian cities had their markets and here much of the business of the city was conducted.

metropolitan - The title used by the head of the Russian church from the conversion of Russia until the establishment of the Patriarchate in 1589.

muzhik - A term used to designate a member of the lower social classes. Often it was used contemptuously to designate the peasant.

Pan (plural, Pani) - Member of the feudal aristocracy of Poland and Lithuania. Some Pani owned thousands of serfs and supplied their own military detachments in time of war. They also held the most important positions in national and regional government.

Pechatnyi dvor - The official Muscovite Printing Office, which was established by Ivan the Terrible in the middle of the 16th century.

pomestie - Inhabited land granted a Muscovite servitor in return for military service. An estate.

Pomorie - The extreme northwest section of Russia that adjoined the White Sea and the Arctic Ocean.

posadskie liudi - Those burghers or townspeople of Muscovy who paid taxes and comprised the middle and lower classes of urban society. The *gosti* were the highest ranking group of this class.

Posol'skii prikaz - Literally, ambassadorial office. The department of the Muscovite government responsible for foreign affairs.

Povolzhie - The Volga region of the Muscovite state.

pristav (plural, pristavy) - A Muscovite police official who performed various functions. In Platonov's context, the official always attached to visiting foreigners or anyone traveling throughout Russia whose actions were suspect. Western ambassadors were met at the border by such an official, who rode at his right during his journey to the capital. The practice seems to have been of Mongol origin and was especially hated by foreigners.

sobor (plural, sobory) - A council meeting or assembly either of ecclesiastics or of social or political groups.

strelets (plural, streltsy) - Literally, shooters. Members of the first regular army units created in Muscovy by Ivan IV. Armed with harquebuses, they comprised an elite group of infantry. They lived in private communities, engaged in business and commerce and were exempt from taxation.

Tsarevich - The son of the Tsar.

Tsarevna - The daughter of the Tsar.

Tsaritsa - The wife of the Tsar.

voevoda - Military governor or governmental head of a town, who was usually high born. The word also meant a general.

yamskaia sloboda - A suburban settlement in which resided post-drivers and other peasants who were responsible for carrying mail, conveying government goods and providing other transportation services.

zemskii sobor - Assembly of the land, or national assembly, of the sixteenth and seventeenth centuries. Originally summoned by Ivan IV in 1549, it often functioned during the Time of Troubles as the highest authority of the land, settling such major issues as war, peace and the selection of a new Tsar.

INDEX

"Accounts of the Days and the Tsars and Saints of Moscow," by Khvorostinin, 63, 67
Akkema, Thielmann, 119
Albert of Lübeck, 2
Alcock, Thomas, 10
Aleksandrova Sloboda, 45
Alevisio, 2
Alexis Mikhailovich, Tsar, 85, 88, 89, 99, 101, 102, 103, 107, 108, 109, 110-111, 112, 117, 122, 123, 133, 138, 152, 154, 155
Alexis, Tsarevich, 128
alms, 59, 105, 129
America, 53
Ankin, Jonathan, 56
Antwerp, 12
Aptekarskii prikaz, 119, 123, 124
Arbatsky section of Moscow, 37, 57
Archangel, 11, 13, 34, 46, 47, 48, 52, 54, 55, 56, 57, 90, 91, 93, 94
Arctic Ocean, 6, 9, 11, 91
Arnd, 6
Asia, 8, 9
Aston, Colonel Arthur, 56
Astrakhan, 9, 10, 26
astrology, 146
Athanasius the Great, 75

Augsburg, 4, 43
Austria, 121
Avvakum, 105, 116, 154
Azarin, Simon, 78, 84-85
Azov, 124

"bait boats," 7
Balkan Peninsula, 58
Baltic Sea, 7, 15, 17, 18, 108, 109
baptism, 60, 68, 87, 153
Baptist, merchant, 43
Barbaro, Josafa, 144
Basil the Great, 75
Bathory, Stefan, King of Poland, 23
beards, 71, 145
Beloborod, Ivan Deval, *see* Van de Walle, Jan
Beloozero, 44
Bergen, 7
Bernzli, 118
"blessing of the waters," 19, 145
boiar duma, 16, 107, 108
boiars, 1, 20-21, 41, 42, 43, 87, 88, 95, 99, 100, 108, 110, 132, 133, 155
Bolotnikov, Ivan, 44, 45, 148, 149
Bolvanovka, 27
Bomel, Elisaeus, 20-21, 145

Bowes, Jerome, 20
Brabant, 90
Briansk, 46
Brückner, Alexander, 122, 156
Brunel, Oliver, 12-13
Brussels, 12
Buchofen, 101
Buczynski, 35, 43
Budny, Simon, 67, 68, 150
Bukhara, 9, 10, 19
bureaucratic absolutism, 109
Burrough, Stephen, 9-10, 12
Bus, Simon, 56-57
Bussow, Conrad, 34, 36, 148
Byzantinism, 30, 50, 144

Caesar, *see* Holy Roman Emperor
Calvin, 67
Caspian Sea, 9, 47
Cathedral of the Assumption, 1-2, 40, 87
Catherine II, Tsarevna, 133
Catholicism, 3, 22, 23, 36, 40, 44, 58, 60, 67, 72, 116, 121, 122, 144, 147, 155
Cellari, 43
Central Asia, 19
Chaadaev, Peter, 133
Chancellor, Richard, 6
Chaney, Richard, 10
Charles, King of Sweden, 46
Charles I, King of England, 116
Charles V, German Emperor, 3-4
Chernigov, 35, 46
China, 6, 8, 9-10, 13
Chodkiewicz, Hetman, 16
Christian III, King of Denmark, 6
Christian IV, King of Denmark, 74
Christianborg, 74
Chudov Monastery, 63

Chuguev, 99
coats of arms, 132
Collier, William, 33
Constantine XI, Byzantine Emperor, 144
Constantinople, 144
Contarini, Ambrogio, 2, 144
Copenhagen, 7, 74
correction of books, 79-82, 124
"Cosmography," 31
Cossacks, 35, 47, 98, 125, 148
Cracow, 27, 43
Crimea, 26 122
Crimean Tatars, 8
Czech lands, 22, 61
Czechowicz, Martin, 67, 68, 150
Czyrzowski, 35

Dal', 150
Danes, 5-6, 18, 28
Danzig, 32
De Meyer, 12
democratization, 100
Denmark, 5, 6, 12, 13, 15, 18, 74, 75
Derbent, 10
deti boiarskie, 57, 94, 97, 98
Digges, Dudley, 55
Dionisius, Archimandrite, 73, 76-82, 83, 84, 85, 86, 106, 151, 152
Dionisius the Areopagite, 75
Dmitrov, 45
Dmitry Ivanovich, Tsar (the Pretender), 35-43, 45, 48, 54, 58, 61, 62, 63, 146, 147, 148, 149
Dnieper River, 126
doctors, 123-124, 156
Dorpat, 10, 16, 17, 22
Dositheos, Patriarch of Jerusalem, 125, 131

Index

Dresden, 61
drugs, 123
Dudin Monastery, 60
Dutch, 11-14, 19, 34, 52, 55, 90, 94, 101, 116, 117
Dvina, see Northern Dvina River

"Edward Bonaventure," 6
Edwards, Arthur, 10
Elizabeth, Queen of England, 20, 26, 34, 54
Emperor, see Holy Roman Emperor
England, 10, 26, 32, 33, 54, 55
Englishmen in Russia, 6-11, 19, 20, 21, 33, 34, 47-48, 54, 55, 89-90, 116, 117, 144
English protectorate in Russia, 47, 48, 54
Eric XIV, King of Sweden, 18
Estland, 14, 18
Estonians, 14
Etat de l'Empire de Russie et Grande Duchè de Moscovia, 37
Eucharist, 66, 68, 156
"Exposition against the Heretics," by Khvorostinin, 67, 68-70, 73

Fathers of the Church, 82, 127
fairs, 8, 93
Fentzel, 118
Feodor Alexeevich, Tsar, 126, 128, 132
Feodor, Deacon, 116
Feodor, Son of Boris Godunov, 35
Filaret Nikitich, 80, 81, 83, 86, 151
Finland, 12
Finns, 18
Fioravanti, Aristotle, 1
Floderan, Adrian, 48, 56

Fogler, Mark, 53, 56
foreign colony in Moscow, 2, 27-29, 34, 43, 96
Forsten, G. V., 17
France, 32, 112
Frederick III, Holy Roman Emperor, 1
freethinking, 31, 68, 71
Frenchmen, 27, 33, 36, 48, 58
Friazin, Anton, 2
"Frozen Sea" (Barents Sea), 91, 153
furs, 2, 9

Galich, 26
Galicia, 43
Germans, 2, 14, 15, 17, 19, 20, 22, 36, 37, 48, 58, 71, 75, 90, 95, 107, 120, 132, 144
Germany, 2, 3, 15, 16, 17, 27, 32, 61
Glukhoi, Arseny, 81, 84, 151
Godunov, Boris, 29, 31-34, 47, 54
Golitsyn, N. V., 147
Golitsyn, Vasily Vasilievich, 111, 113-114, 122
Golubtsov, A., 150
Gordon, Patrick, 121-122, 138, 156
Gosiewski, 61, 150
Goslar, 4
gostinaia sotnia, 119, 155
gostinye dvory, 27, 56, 91, 117
Gottfried, Johann, 112
grain, 90, 91, 118
Gramotin, Ivan Tarasievich, 61-62, 70, 149-150
Grand Master of Livonia, 17
Grecophilism, 81, 82, 84
Greek Orthodoxy, 59, 129-131
"green stalls," 124
Gregory XIII, Pope, 25

Greeks, 2, 58, 81, 82, 83, 84, 85, 103, 104, 105, 128-131, 137, 139, 152, 156
Grigoriev, Nikifor Alferievich, 33
guards, 36, 101
Guilderstern, Axel, 28, 32
Gulf of Riga, 108
gunpowder, 37
Gustav, Swedish Prince, 32

Hamburg, 58, 61, 90, 117
Hamel, J., 145
Hamilton, Evdokiia Grigorievna, 112, 122
Hans, Duke of Holstein, 28, 32, 147
Hanse, *see* Hanseatic League
Hanseatic League, 4, 5, 14, 17, 18
Henry IV, King of France, 36
heresy, 30, 50, 58, 63, 65-70, 71, 72, 73, 81, 87-88, 152, 153, 156
Hermogen, 63, 67, 77, 150, 151
History of the Great Prince of Moscow, by Kurbsky, 27
Holland, 13, 53, 90, 118
Holstein, 57, 58
Holy Roman Emperor, 5, 15, 36, 62, 112, 144
Holy Week, 65
Horsey, Sir Jerome, 19, 21, 27, 145
"Hospital of Feodor Rtishchev," 105
"How the Queen Cut Off the Head of King Holofernes," 112
"Hundred Chapters" *(Stoglav),* 79, 80, 151
Hungarians, 58
Huntingdonshire, 33

icon painters, 76, 125

icons, 67, 71, 76, 87, 115, 130, 132
Ikonnikov, V. S., 154
Ingles, Peter, 112
India, 6, 8
"Instructive Gospel," by Trankvillion-Stavrovetsky, 72
Iona, Metropolitan, 80, 81
Irina Mikhailovna, Tsarevna, 86
iron ore, 8
iron-works, 8
Italians, 2, 14
Italy, 2, 129, 130
Ivan Alexeevich, Tsar, 125
Ivan III, Tsar, 1, 144
Ivan IV, the Terrible, Tsar, 3, 5, 6, 10, 14, 15, 16, 17, 19-27, 31, 32, 33, 34, 47, 107, 145, 146
Ivangorod, 17, 71
Izmailovo, 137

James I, King of England, 47, 54, 56
Jena, 2
Jenkinson, Anthony, 9-10, 12, 19
Jesuits, 23-25, 36, 114, 116
Joachim, Patriarch, 127, 131
John of Damascus, 75
Johnson, Richard, 10
Jordan ceremony, 145
Joseph, Patriarch, 95
Josephus, Flavius, 75
Judaizers, 30, 146

kabbala, 146
Kalb, Adrian, 16
Kaliazin, 45
Kaluga, 118
Kama River, 15
Kandalaksha, 12
Kanin Nos, 9
Kapterev, N. F., 129, 156

Index

Karamzin, 145
Kashkin, N. N., 154
Katyrev-Rostovsky, Prince Ivan Mikhailovich, 73, 156
Kazan, 5, 10, 15, 90, 148
Kazvin, 10
Kellermann, 118
Kholmogory, 6, 8, 9, 10, 12, 19, 47, 54, 55, 56, 57, 90
Khvorostinin, Prince Ivan Andreevich, 62-70, 73, 102, 149
Kiev, 35, 60, 105, 125, 131
Kilburger, 117
Kirillov Monastery, 65, 66
Kitaigorod, 8, 57, 117
Klementiev, Simanka, 56
Kliuchevsky, V. O., 84, 109, 113, 154, 155
Knutsen, 37, 147
"Kokui," 29, 146
Kola Inlet, 9, 11, 12, 13, 87
Kolomenskoe, 136
Koshkin family, 149
Kostroma, 16, 44, 53, 90
Kotoshikhin, Grigory Karpovich, 114-115, 116, 155
Kozlovsky, I. P., 154
Kremlin, 2, 19, 28, 35, 37, 39, 40, 42, 43, 57, 63, 88, 132, 134, 136, 151
Krizhanich, Yury, 105, 154
Krosno, 43
Kruse, Elert, 15-16
Ksenia, daughter of Boris Godunov, 32
Kurbatov, 149
Kurbsky, Prince Andrei, 26, 27
Kursk, 99

Ladoga, Lake, 8
Laishev, 15
Lampozhnia, 8, 9
Lapland, 12
Latvians, 14
Lawicki, 36
Lefort, Franz, 138
Leipzig, 61
Leslie, Alexander, 57, 58
"Lesovik," 157
Likhach, E. A., 154
Likhudy brothers, 131
Lisowski, Alexander, 56, 148
Lithuania, 2, 5, 6, 16, 60, 65, 68, 72, 107, 149
Lithuanians, 15, 20, 22, 37, 38, 42, 44, 45, 48, 59, 98
Little Russians, see Ukrainians
Liubimenko, N. N., 54
Livland, 14, 15
Livonia, 4, 5, 6, 14-18, 19
Livonian War, 14-18
Livonians, 22, 26, 29
"Logic," 31
London, 8
"Lord States-General of the Netherlands," see Holland
Lower Reaches, 46, 148
Lübeck, 2, 4, 18, 22, 32, 58, 61, 115
Luther, 23, 67, 75
Lutheranism, 51
Lutherans, 73, 75
Lykov, Ivan, 27
Lykov, Matvei, 26
Lykov, Mikhail Matveevich, 26
Lyskovo, 83

Magnus, Duke, 146
Mangazeia, 9
Mangyshlak Peninsula, 9
Margariti, 75, 151
Margeret, Jacques, 29, 36, 48, 148
Maria Il'inichna, Tsaritsa, 105

Marselis, Christian, 118
Marselis family, 118, 119
Marselis, Leonty, 118
Marselis, Peter, 118
Massa, Isaac, 34, 47, 52, 53, 61-62, 65, 148
Matveev, Artamon Sergeevich, 111-113, 122
Maxim the Confessor, 8
Maxim the Greek, 82, 152
Maximilian, Habsburg Emperor, 48
medicine, 123-124
Medvedev, Silvester, 131
Melnishnaia, 57
Menezius, Paul, 121
mercantilism, 109
mercenaries, 45, 46, 50, 56, 58
merchants: *Dutch,* 11-14, 18, 47, 50, 53, 90, 117; *English,* 6-11, 18, 33-34, 47, 50, 53, 89-90, 117; *foreign,* 33, 43, 50, 51, 91, 92, 93, 95; *German,* 2, 19, 43, 90, 91; *Greek,* 59; *Livonian,* 19; *Persian,* 9; *Polish,* 2; *Russian,* 89, 90, 91, 92, 93, 94, 98, 100; *Tatar,* 9
Merrick, John, 47, 54, 55
Merrick, William, 54
Meyerberg, German ambassador, 120
Mezen River, 8
Miasnitskaia section of Moscow, 95
Michael Feodorovich, Tsar, 47, 49, 53, 54, 55, 56, 58, 62, 63, 74, 99, 117, 123, 153, 156
Mikhailov, Ivan, 66
Mikulin, Grigory Ivanovich, 33
Milan, 43
Miliukov, Paul, 133, 140
Miloslavsky family, 134, 136, 139
Miloslavsky, Ivan D., 101

Mniszech, Marina, 38-40, 42, 147
Mniszech, Yury, 38
Moldavians, 58
Monastery of the Assumption, 39
Monastery of Joseph of Volokolamsk, 63
Monastery of Staritsa, 77
monks, 59, 60, 61, 136, 137, 139
"Moravian Brethren," 22
Moravians, 33, 35
Moskva River, 27
Moslems, 59
Mstislavsky, 84
Multiane, 58
Murmansk, 7, 11, 13, 19
Muscovy Company, 53
mutiny of 1648, 99-101
muzhik, 100

Narova River, 17
Narva, 10, 11, 17, 18, 19, 115
"Narva sailing," 17-18
Naryshkin family, 122
Nasedka, Ivan, 73-76, 78, 81, 84, 87
Nashchoka, 107
Natalia Kirillovna, mother of Peter the Great, 133, 134, 136
Neronov, Ivan, 78, 83-84, 85, 86, 152
Neuville, 113
Neva River, 108
New Testament, 75
Niemojewski, 28, 63, 147
Nikita, priest, 87
Nikon, Patriarch, 82, 94-95, 100, 102, 104, 105, 125, 128, 129, 130, 152, 154
Nizhnii Novgorod, 16, 45, 83, 90
Nogai Tatars, 65
North Africa, 9
Northern Dvina River, 6, 7, 8, 9,

Index

Northern Dvina River, cont'd. 11, 13, 18, 19, 34, 50, 52, 91, 152
Norway, 7, 12
Novaia Zemlia, 9
Novgorod, 3, 8, 12, 17, 19, 30, 45, 61, 146
Novomeshchansky, 112
Nuremberg, 61

Ob River, 9, 12
Ogorodniki, 57
Oka River, 60
Old Testament, 75
Olearius (Adam Oelschläger), 57, 71, 95
Onega, Lake, 8, 12
"On Icons," 74
"On the Icons and the Cross," 73
"On Iconoclasts and All Evil Heresies," by Katyrev-Rostovsky, 73
"On the Resurrection of the Dead," 68
Opochka, 107
oprichniki, 145
oprichnina, 16, 145
orators, 126
Ordin-Nashchokin, Afanasy Lavrentievich, 103, 106-111, 154, 155
Ordin-Nashchokin, Denis Gavrilovich, 107
Orel, 35
Orthodox Academy, 131
Orthodoxy, 3, 22, 23, 24, 40, 50, 60, 63, 64-70, 73, 87, 115, 119, 121, 127, 144, 147, 155
Ostrov, 107

Padua, University of, 131
Paerle, 147
Paisios, Patriarch of Jerusalem, 59

Paleologos, Sophia, 2, 144
Palestine, 9
Parcet, Jean, 33
Paris, 12
Pavlov-Sil'vansky, N. P., 157
Pechatnyi dvor, 59, 72, 77, 79, 80, 81, 82
Pechenga Bay, 11, 12, 13
Pechora, 8, 9, 12, 53
Penzner, Franz, 57
Persia, 2, 10, 55
Peter the Great, Tsar, 52, 105, 109, 119, 122, 123, 125, 132-141
Petrarch, 44
Petrei, 148
Peza River, 8
Philip, merchant of Ivangorod, 71
physicians, 123-124
Pinega River, 8
Pisemsky, Feodor, 26
"plank boats," 7
"playmate" company, 137
Pokrovka Gates, 96
Pokrovskaia section of Moscow, 57, 95
Poland, 2, 5, 14, 22, 26, 35, 44, 46, 51, 55, 57, 59, 60, 68, 72, 80, 81, 108, 109, 120, 150, 151
Poles, 35-43, 44, 45, 46, 47, 48, 56, 57, 59, 61, 62, 64, 67, 79, 85, 121, 148, 150, 151
Polish-Lithuanian Commonwealth, *see* Poland
Polish vogue, 132
Polish War of Tsar Alexis, 85, 125
Polotsky, Semen, 126-127, 128, 131, 132, 136
Pommerening, 94
Pomorie, 8, 19, 46, 91, 118
Pope, 5, 24-25, 42, 130
Poppel, Nicholas, 1-3, 144

posadskie liudi, 100, 101
Posol'skii prikaz, 88, 89, 106, 107, 108, 114, 119
Possevino, Antonio, 23-25, 26
postal service, 118, 119
Povents, 8
Povolzhie, 45
Pozharsky, Dmitry, 47, 48, 56, 63, 148
Prechistensky section of Moscow, 37
Preobrazhenskoe, 134, 135, 137
Preobrazhensky regiment, 137
Pressburg, 137
Pretender, *see* Dmitry Ivanovich, Tsar
Pretender, second, 45, 61
prisoners, foreign, in Russia, 14-18, 19, 22, 44, 58
pristav, 2, 23, 28, 66
privateers, 18
Procurator General, 140, 141
Protestantism, 4, 16, 22, 23, 28, 32, 36, 51, 58, 71, 72, 73, 74, 75, 115, 116, 150
Prussians, 62
Pskov, 30, 106, 107, 108, 109, 146, 155
Pudozhem Mouth of the Dvina River, 13
Puritan movement, 33
Pustozersk, 8, 9
Putivl, 35
Pypin, A. N., 82

Radogoshch, 26
Randolph, Thomas, 21-22
Rasmussen, 6
rationalism, 30, 51, 61
Razin, Stenka, 102
Razmysl, 6
Reformation, 150
Renaissance, 30

Reval, 4, 17-18, 114
Rzhevitin, *see* Dionisius, Archimandrite
Riazan, 16
Riga, 108
Rode, Carsten, 18
Rokyta, Jan, 22-23
Romanov family, 149
Romanov, Filaret, *see* Filaret Nikitich
Rome, 4, 44, 122
ropewalk, 8
Rose Island, 7, 13
Rostov, 44
Rozynski, Prince Roman, 45
Rtishchev, Feodor Mikhailovich, 103-106, 111, 125, 154
Rudolph, Holy Roman Emperor, 42
Russell, William, 47
Russian Public Library, 68
Ruffo, Marco, 2
Rzhev, 76

Saint Andrew's Monastery, 60, 104, 105
Saint Nicholas of Karelia, 6, 13
Saint Nicholas the Wonderworker, 41
Saint Paul, 23
saints, lives of, 84, 106, 127
Samarkand, 10
Sapieha, Jan Peter, 45
Sapieha, Lithuanian chancellor, 149
Savva, V. I., 146
Scandinavia, 12, 17
schism, 102, 128, 129, 154
Schleizing, 120
Schlitte, Hans, 3-5
Scotland, 121
Semenovsky regiment, 137
Senate, 140, 141

Index

Serbs, 58
Servetus, 67, 68
Shah, 10
Shakhovskoi, Prince Semen I., 64-65, 86-88, 102, 103, 152
Shaklovity, 135
Shaw, James, 47-48
Shchelkalov, Andrei, 20
Shemaka, 10
Shevelev, Ioann Vasilievich, *see* Nasedka, Ivan
Shuisky, Vasily Ivanovich, Tsar, 41, 44, 45, 50, 63, 148, 151
Siberia, 12, 13, 91, 145, 155
Sigismund Augustus, King of Poland, 26, 39, 42, 46, 62, 150, 151
Simeon the Proud, 107
Sivtsevy Vrazhok section of Moscow, 57
Sixth Ecumenical Council, 64
Skopin-Shuisky, Prince Mikhail V., 45
Slavinetsky, Epiphany, 127-128
Smith, T., 56
Smolensk, 7
Socinianism, 68, 150
Socinus, Faustus, 150
Socinus, Laelius, 150
Solario, Pietro, 2
Soloviev, S. M., 112, 133, 156
Solovki Islands, 8
Sol'vychegodsk, 88, 98
Sophia Alexeevna, Tsarevna, 114, 122, 128, 131, 134, 136, 139
Spain, 53, 112
Speransky, M. N., 30, 31, 146
Stadnicki, Martin, 37, 38, 41, 44, 147
Stadnicki, Peter, 44
Staritsa, 77
Starodub, 5
Stashevsky, E., 156

"Statement to the Lutherans," by Nasedka, 74-75
Stockholm, 114
Stoglav, see "Hundred Chapters"
Stolbovo, treaty of, 93
streltsy, 44, 99, 100, 101, 133-135, 136
strigol'niki, 30, 146
Stroganovs, 12, 13, 145
Sukhanov, Arseny, 130
Surgeons, 123-124, 156
Sweden, 46, 58, 94, 100, 107, 108, 115, 120
Swedes, 18, 26, 45, 46, 47, 54, 99, 100, 108, 114-115, 121
Syromiatnaia, 57

"Tale of the Devastation of the Muscovite State," by Azarin, 85
Tatars, 4, 144
Tatar yoke, 30
Taube, Johann, 15-16
Tavriz, 10
Tavzin, treaty of, 93
theologians, 72, 87, 104, 127, 156
Theophanes, Patriarch of Jerusalem, 78, 81
Third Rome, 85
Time of Troubles, 35-48, 49, 50, 52, 53, 55, 58, 59, 60, 62, 71, 72, 73, 79, 85, 89, 91, 97, 98, 100
Timofeev, Ivan, 21, 25
Trankvillion-Stavrovetsky, Kirill, 72
"translations," 79
transubstantiation, 127
Trinity-St. Sergius Monastery, 66, 73, 76-80, 82, 83, 84, 134-135, 149
Trondheim, 7
Tsvetaev, D. V., 57, 149, 151

Tula, 35, 118, 119
Turkey, 9
Turks, 4, 5, 59, 130, 144
Tushino, 44, 45, 47, 61
Tver, 45
Tverskaia section of Moscow, 57

Uglich, 17, 32
Ugriane, 58
Ukraine, 35, 104, 108, 124-128
Ukrainians, 44, 51, 60, 85, 104, 105, 124-128, 137, 139, 152, 156
Ul'ianov, Ivan, 149
Ulozhenie, 100, 154
undermining, 5
Uniates, 60
Unskaia Inlet, 7
Urusov, Ivan Ivanovich, 76
Ust Tsilma, 8, 9

Vaigacha Island, 9
Vandeman, 37
Van de Walle, Jan, 13, 14, 20
Van Klenk family, 117-118
Van Klenk, George, 53, 56
Van Salingen, 12
Vardohüys, 12
Varvarka, 8, 54
Velikie Luki, 46
Velikii Ustiug, 99
Venice, 2, 131
Viazemy, 41
Viaz'ma, 46
Vinius, Andrei, 118
Vinius, Andrei Andreevich, 119
Vladimir, 16
Vlasiev, Afanasy, 38, 41
Voin, son of A. L. Ordin-Nashchokin, 110-111
Volga River, 9, 15, 45, 47, 55
Volkhov River, 8

Vologda, 7, 8, 19, 44, 45, 46, 47, 54, 61, 90, 91
Voloshane, 58
Von Dam, Heinrich, 58
Von Eberfeld, Caspar, 16, 22
Vonifatiev, Stefan, 83, 104, 152
Vyborg, 17
Vychegda, 8
Vyg River, 8
Vyluzgin, Elizar, 19

Waldemar, Danish Prince, 86-88, 153
Wallachians, 58
Watts, William, 56
Western Dvina River, 108
Wetterman, Pastor, 16, 22
white cowl, 81, 152
White Sea, 7, 47, 53
wine, 29
Wladyslaw, Polish Prince, 57
Wren, George, 10

Yagra Island, 7
yamskaia sloboda, 77
Yaroslavl, 12, 19, 44, 47, 53, 54, 61, 64, 90, 91
Yauza River, 28, 96
Yugoria, 9
Yuriev, 149

Zablocki, 65
Zakharin, 149
Zaleshin, 23
Zaozersky, A. I., 154
Zemlianoi Gorod, 96
zemskii sobor, 48, 94
Zlatostrui, 75, 151
Zobninovsky, David Feodorovich, *see* Dionisius, Archimandrite
Zotov, 136

Platonov, Sergei Fedorovich, 1860-1933.
  Moscow and the West [by] S. F. Platonov.
Translated and edited by Joseph L. Wieczynski.
Introduction by Serge A. Zenkovsky. [Hattiesburg,
Miss.] Academic International, 1972.
    xxiii, 171 p. map. 21 cm. (Russian series, v. 9)
   Translation of Москва и Запад (title romanized:
Moskva i Zapad) Leningrad, 1925.
   Bibliographical footnotes.

   1. Russia-Civilization-Occidental influences.
  I. Wieczynski, Joseph L., ed. and tr. II. Title.
DK67.P5513
ISBN: O-87569-019-X   914.7   72-142000